PAUL McLAUGHLIN

To Wilhelm !
Welcome !

Welcome to

Reality

Now You Know®

90 Sheppard Avenue East, Suite 300
North York, Ontario M2N 6X1
Tel: (416) 224-2248; 1-800-268-4522
Fax: (416) 224-2243; 1-800-461-4131
http://www.ca.cch.com

Published by CCH Canadian Limited

Important Disclaimer: This publication is sold with the understanding that (1) the authors and editors are not responsible for the results of any actions taken on the basis of information in this work, nor for any errors or omissions; and (2) the publisher is not engaged in rendering legal, accounting or other professional services. The publisher, and the authors and editors, expressly disclaim all and any liability to any person, whether a purchaser of this publication or not, in respect of anything and of the consequences of anything done or omitted to be done by any such person in reliance, whether whole or partial, upon the whole or any part of the contents of this publication. If legal advice or other expert assistance is required, the services of a competent professional person should be sought.

Ownership of Trade Mark

Canadian Cataloguing in Publication Data

McLaughlin, Paul, 1946-
    Welcome to reality : a new lawyer's guide to success

ISBN 1-55141-354-X

1. Practice of law.   2. Law offices.   I. Title.

KE335.M34 2000   340'.068   C00-930104-6

 Typeset and printed in Canada by CCH Canadian Limited.

Welcomes *you* to

Reality

Congratulations on beginning your new law career!

We at CCH are pleased to present you with this practical and enjoyable book at this important time in your career. *Welcome to Reality* will help you successfully make the transition from the academic arena to the demanding and challenging world of legal practice.

This book is one example of CCH's commitment to provide you with the information resources you need to succeed – now and throughout your law career.

Research tools from CCH are available via the internet, CD Rom, looseleaf subscriptions, and bound books – whatever format you need for ready reference and to supplement your legal education.

These products cover many specialized areas of law, including securities, corporate, commercial, real estate, family, insurance, labour, estates, transportation, and others.

For more information please contact us.
Or call us toll free at 1-800-268-4522.
Fax 1-800-461-4131
Visit us at www.ca.cch.com

Welcome to Reality: A New Lawyer's Guide to Success

Table of Contents

Canadian Lawyers Leave Their Real Estate Hassles On Our Doorstep

Fewer problems. More business.

Lawyers work hard closing real estate transactions for their clients. They juggle many files at once trying to anticipate and pre-empt potential problems. Sometimes things go smoothly, sometimes they don't. First Canadian Title can help real estate lawyers close transactions faster and with fewer hassles, so that they have more time to do more business.

Our title insurance eliminates the need and expense for an up-to-date survey or real property report, and in most provinces many time consuming and costly off title searches. It satisfies lenders, and it can protect buyers against closing delays.

One of the reasons Canadian lawyers call us first is that we make the process easy. They get the same dedicated service from our professionally trained staff whether they contact us by phone, fax or internet.

First Canadian Title introduced title insurance to Canada in 1991 and is the industry leader. We have an established and credible claims history. We are backed by the world leader in real estate related financial and information services. And, thanks to Canadian lawyers our title insurance protected over 100,000 real estate transactions in Canada last year.

For more information about title insurance call First Canadian Title at: 1-800-307-0370.

FIRST CANADIAN TITLE

Title Insurance • Home Closing Services
Home Warranty • Real Estate Tax Services

GET PLUGGED IN!

Document Assembly
for the
Law Office

A Self-Instruction Guide using WordPerfect for
Windows (and nothing else)
by
Paul McLaughlin

*"Learn how to create simple, effective and flexible
document assembly systems using the power of
WordPerfect"*

Available over the Internet for $29.95
For more information, point your browser to
http://www.compusmart.ab.ca/dogonit/docasmbl
or call (780) 922-6625

Dogonit Enterprises
dogonit@compusmart.ab.ca

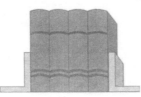

Preface

I remember meeting with Suzanne Tyson, Director, New Product Acquisitions, and Cheryl Finch, Senior Developmental Editor, at the CCH Canadian offices in Toronto in the summer of 1998. In the middle of a conversation about another project, someone—I don't remember who—mentioned the idea of a book of tips for new lawyers. There was an almost audible click in the room. Suzanne shifted into acquisitions mode and said, "What a great project!" Cheryl shifted into editor mode and said, "Yes, let's do it!" I shifted into writer mode, a table of contents started to form in my mind, and I said, "Okay, let's do it!"

When I started writing, the draft poured out. I never once suffered from a writer's block during this entire project. The complete first draft went to CCH in early January, and by the end of March, the book was ready for the printer.

I was able to complete this project because of the tremendous help I received from many people.

Suzanne and Cheryl were terrific.

My family was extremely supportive. They put up with my sneaking off to my den and losing myself in my computer instead of heading off to the mall for the Boxing Week sales. I owe a special debt of thanks to each of them: to Andrew, who is entering law school this fall, for suggesting the mountain-climbing metaphor; to Erica and Kirsten for reading the manuscript and providing their very insightful comments; and to Mike for his complete faith that his Dad could do this thing.

My deepest gratitude goes to Carol, my beloved wife, my best friend, my most demanding editor and critic, on whom I rely for my inspiration and to whom I dedicate this book.

Finally, I have to give special thanks to my good friends Maurice Dumont and Diane Ellis, for reading and commenting on my drafts.

And, of course, the mistakes are all mine.

March, 1999
Sherwood Park, Alberta

Introduction

Welcome to the real world!

And congratulations! When you graduated from law school, you made it to the top of a hill. Now you can look back down the hill and can see the many milestones that mark your path to the crest. You are entitled to take a moment to glory in your achievement.

Okay, that's long enough. Turn around, and you can see that you are actually at the foot of a mountain—in fact, a whole range of mountains with many different elevations and ridges and lookouts and innumerable routes to many summits. You may well spend the rest of your working life in these mountains, so it's a good idea to start figuring out their geography.

New rules

The day you walked out of your last law school exam, the rules changed forever.

Until then, your primary objective was to graduate. You reached your goal by performing well in class, on written assignments and on exams.

Now, you have many goals to choose from, and many complex, interweaving pathways you can take to reach them. You also have many obstacles preventing you from arriving at your chosen destinations. But no matter what your goals are, and no matter what paths you choose to reach them, the fundamental rule you now live by is this:

To succeed, you must ethically make a positive contribution to your clients and your legal organization.

Clients: all consumers of legal services, including clients in the traditional sense, other departments in a corporation and other departments or agencies in a government

Let's look at this rule more closely. It implies that your success depends on satisfying your **clients**, the **legal organization** in which you work and your **professional licencing body**.

You make a positive contribution to your **clients** by rendering legal services that solve their legal problems in ways that meet their legal and psychological needs. Meeting their legal needs is the basic service; meeting their psychological needs is a **collateral benefit** that encourages them to become repeat clients and to refer their friends and colleagues.

Legal organization: any organization that provides legal services through lawyers, including law firms (solo, small, medium and large), law departments in business corporations, government offices that provide legal services and nonprofit organizations that render legal services. Even a solo practitioner works in an organization. The solo practice without staff is a one-person organization in which the practitioner fills all the roles.

You make a positive contribution to your **organization** by keeping your clients happy, but that is just a start. In these competitive times, no one has resources to waste, and if you want to become a good investment for a legal services organization, you must contribute to its ability to achieve its goals. In other words, your success depends on whether you can deliver what your organization wants from you.

You also have to satisfy your **professional licensing body**—in Canada, your law society and in the United States, your state bar—by acting ethically in everything you do to satisfy clients and the legal organization in which you work.

Collateral benefit: the client's feeling of peace of mind. From a marketing perspective, the collateral benefits are often more important than the technical services.

How this book can help you

This book focuses on the practical knowledge, skills, attitudes and habits that will launch your career on a solid footing, no matter how you choose to use your legal training. It is designed to help you lay down solid foundations for long-term success during your first two years out in the real world.

Each chapter contains plenty of helpful tips. Pick the tips you like and commit yourself to implementing as many of them as you can. Schedule yourself to read this book again every three months over the next two years. Each time through, you will find more ideas you want to implement, and in two years, you will be well on your way toward achieving success, however you define it for yourself.

> You can use your legal training in an ever-expanding array of career paths that don't involve practicing law in the traditional sense. See Chapter 11, "Planning Your Career".

So, welcome to the foot of the mountain. It's a great place to start. If you work hard and smart, you'll soon find yourself looking down from the first lookout, smiling at your own achievements.

Chapter 1

How to Make Friends with Your Files

No matter how you use your law degree, files will play a huge role in your work life. You start to really feel like a real lawyer when you get your first file; if you work full-time, you probably spend more time with your files than with your family or colleagues; and you'll know you are no longer a practicing lawyer when you don't have any more files to work on.

Files are an important **physical presence** in a lawyer's work life. When you draft a document, the file is right there on your desk. When you go to court or a meeting, you want the file with you at all times. When you meet with your clients, you bring the file not only for your own convenience, but also because it's comforting for clients to see a tangible manifestation of the work you are doing on their behalf.

Files are also an **organizational unit** for a lawyer's work. You start a new matter by opening a file. As long as the file is open, it represents work you have done and work you have yet to do. When the file is closed, the matter is considered complete and you can move on to other work, other files.

Your files are proof that **your work matters to someone**, that practicing law is not an academic exercise, that lawyers exist to solve the real problems of real people in the real world. If you brought in the work yourself, it's even sweeter—the file is evidence that someone out there wants you to be their lawyer!

> 66 All I really need to know about how to live and what to do and how to be I learned in kindergarten. Wisdom was not at the top of the graduate-school mountain, but there in the sand pile at Sunday School. These are [two of] the things I learned: . . . Put things back where you found them. Clean up your own mess. 99
>
> — ROBERT FULGHUM, *All I Really Need to Know I Learned in Kindergarten*

You can use a file as a prop: when you want to threaten to leave a meeting, pick up your file and slam it into your briefcase.

Your files are **records that may become public.** They document on paper (and increasingly, electronically) the steps taken to complete a matter. Your client expects you to keep notes of all significant events as the matter progresses, and if it ever becomes necessary to prove what occurred, your file may become evidence of what happened, subject to the client's consent.

> Many lawyers use the physical presence of their files on their desks (and on the floor and every other horizontal surface in their offices) to remind them of pending work. They get anxious when their files are not physically present and visible. This is not good personal practice management, but it shows the deep physical attachment many lawyers have to their files.

Your files remind you that **you are part of an organization.** This, admittedly, can be positive or negative: your files may represent exciting challenges and opportunities offered by your organization, or they may threaten to crush you in an avalanche of tedium.

Your files are a **repository for the value of your work**, an asset of your organization. If you are in private practice, the work is billed out and converted into money. In a corporate practice, your work is an indirect contributor to the profitability of other departments. In a government or nonprofit practice, your work is a manifestation of the organization's efforts to spend its resources to achieve its goals, whatever they may be.

All this means that your files are a major element in your experience of practicing law, so it is a good idea to develop a positive relationship with them.

"Lawyer, meet file. File, meet lawyer. I think you two will get along."

Your files can be friends or enemies, and believe me, you are much better off if they are your friends. As friends, they can provide you with intellectual challenge, the opportunity to help people, advancement, money—whatever it is you hope to get out of being a lawyer. If you disrespect or neglect them, they can drive you crazy, oppress you, plummet you into depression, suck you into malpractice, impoverish you—everything you hope **not** to get out of practicing law.

> There is a rough correlation between the thickness of a file and the amount it is worth.

If files were people, they would be neat freaks. It's as though they become irritable when you let them get messy. At night, when no one is looking, they pass important documents around so no one can find them. Sometimes, they spit documents out in the hope that no one will be able to track them down.

It's easy to help your files overcome this nasty behavior. All you have to do is develop three orderly personal work habits:

- **Nail everything down.** There are many ways to do this. A common one is to use corner spikes, but any method that prevents paper from spilling out of the file will do.

- **Divide your files into categories.** Some common categories include correspondence, drafts, executed documents, client documents, court documents, law and research. In small files, you can use corner spikes to separate the categories, but in larger files you should use subfiles. You can also use ring binders or multi-part file folders—whatever works for you to keep the paper organized.

• **Keep your filing current.** The filing is your responsibility, not your assistant's, even if you delegate the actual work. It takes discipline and coordination to keep on top of it. Don't use your desk to store material that should be in the files. And don't use incoming letters to remind you to work on a file.

> Your support staff will appreciate everything you do to help keep the filing up to date.

> Did you hear the one about the 95-year-old legal assistant who had vowed, at 65, to retire as soon as the filing was caught up!

Another thing about files—they hate it when you procrastinate. They don't want you to damage your reputation with clients, your employer, the courts, other lawyers or anyone else who depends on you to get your work done on time. Even files for which there are no specific deadlines grow anxious if nothing is happening. Neglected files are capable of the most exquisite torture. They intrude on your thoughts at the most inopportune times to remind you of your failure to meet your commitments. They grind away at your self-confidence. And they drive your stress level through the roof. In extreme conditions, they can destroy you.

> An incomplete file is dangerous, even if it looks good. At best, it can cause you to waste a lot of valuable time searching for errant pieces of paper. At worst, it can result in poor decisions based on incomplete information.

The best way to deal with this unpleasant tendency of files is simple to say but hard to do: stay on top of your work. See Chapter 7, "Time Management", for more ideas on how to do this.

The last thing you need to know about files is that they have very active, though secret, social lives.

The Secret Life of Files

Working late in my office one night, I heard a faint beat of dance music and a tinkle of laughter coming from a filing cabinet. The files in the cabinet were having a party—dancing, drinking, an all-round wild time!

Suddenly I was noticed and in an instant, they were just files again.

"Whoa!" I said to myself. "You've been working too hard."

Then I heard a throat-clearing noise from my desk. I turned and a file that been gathering dust on the corner of my desk for a very long time spoke.

"Do you know what you're doing to us?" it whined. "Every night when you go home, there's a fantastic party in the filing cabinet. But I've been stuck here for three whole months and I never get to be with my friends!"

"I didn't know that," I protested.

"You just leave me here, month after month. It's so-o-o-o lonely. I try to torment you so you'll put me back with my friends, but it's just not working!"

"Well, I didn't know!" I protested again.

"Well, du-uh! Why, you don't even know the first rule about how to organize your work!"

"What's that?"

"Work from lists, not from files!!"

"What do you mean?"

"I can't believe you don't know this. Every day, you get a list of the files marked for review that day. Not the files themselves, a list. If you have an electronic calendar, you get a printout of your current To-Do list. You go through the list and immediately set a new target date for the files that will not get done that day. You use the list to give instructions to your staff, like 'Send follow-up letter.' Then you prioritize the rest of the list and pull only the files you will be working on. Work through them in order of priority. Before you go home, set new dates for the files you haven't completed and put them back in the filing cabinet (it's party time!)."

As I absorbed this information, one of the other files spoke in a worried voice. "Oh, my!" it said. "There's going to be big trouble. It's against the rules to tell you these things, you know."

"What a stupid rule! Who made it?"

"The Legal Malpractice Insurance files," came the reply. "It's the way they ensure the survival of their species!"

Using files to make a good impression

Your files also want you to make a good impression.

A good deal of a lawyer's work is done away from the direct observation of clients—drafting, researching, negotiating, talking with other lawyers on the phone, discussing cases with colleagues. In fact, some of your most important work—reflecting, analyzing, planning, strategizing—is inherently invisible. Yet experts say that the perception of effort is one of the most important factors in client satisfaction. How do you show effort when so much of your work can't be seen?

Clients reach conclusions about your qualities as a lawyer by extrapolating from the visible to the invisible. The condition of your files becomes a symbol of your skills and your attitude toward them and their problems. Messy, disorganized files project carelessness, while neat, well-organized files convey concern, competence and attention to detail.

Clients and others don't necessarily make conscious judgments about the condition of your files; rather, their subconscious observations blend with many other impressions and crystallize into an opinion subtly affecting how much they trust you.

Your clients also use the condition of your files to draw conclusions about how your mind works. If you are chronically unable to find what you need in your file, they become anxious. They wonder if your mind is similarly jumbled. They fret over whether you will be able to recall that critical fact or point of law you need to win their case in court.

On the other hand, if you can always put your hands on file material that you need, clients feel safer because they can literally see that you have a disciplined, orderly mind.

The condition of your files will be a factor in your performance evaluation. Files that look out of control raise concerns
about whether you have the personal practice management
skills needed to become a valuable contributor to the organization. For example,

- If you are not available, could someone else pick up
  your files and run with them?
- Do your files make the kind of impression the organization wants?
- Do your poor work habits create unnecessary risks for
  the organization?

In an effort to appear
"folksy", some lawyers let
their offices and files get
messy. They say it makes their
clients feel more comfortable
to see that their lawyer is a little sloppy and casual, just like
they are. This is a legitimate
marketing strategy **if the
lawyer is in fact in complete
control of the practice and is
just putting on an act,** but
not if it's just a rationaliza-
tion.

Other lawyers and judges notice the condition of your
files, so your reputation in the legal community, and con-
sequently your effectiveness as a lawyer, is influenced by
the messages they send.

Setting standards

Here is a proposed standard for file maintenance:

**My clients can come in at any time and look through their
files without their condition or contents embarrassing me.**

Your files should contain:

Your files should **not** contain
negative personal observations
about your clients or other
parties. You really don't want
the client or another lawyer to
read that you think the client
is a "lying, no-good SOB".

1. Clear identification of the client and matter
2. Name, address and contact numbers for the client
3. Terms of the retainer, including the scope of work requested and the terms of payment
4. Limitation deadlines
5. Checklists
6. Copies of all outgoing correspondence and originals of all incoming correspondence
7. Hard copies of important e-mail, sent and received
8. Transcriptions of, or memos to file summarizing important voice-mail messages
9. Notes on telephone and other conversations detailing information received, advice given and instructions conveyed
10. Notes on court appearances and meetings attended
11. Drafts of documents, at least until they are finalized by being executed, filed or registered (some firms retain drafts indefinitely as part of the record of the matter)
12. Executed documents, including, in litigation files, a complete set of the court documents
13. Legal research
14. Copies of statements of account

15. A full accounting of all trust transactions
16. In complex files, a short summary of the case on the
    inside left file cover for quick reference

Well, what should I do?

When you start working in a law office, you are expected to
follow the file organization methods already in place. This can
be good or bad, depending on the culture of the office.

In some offices, the files are neat and organized. If you find
yourself in this kind of office, do your best to absorb the good
work habits of those around you.

In other offices, the files are a disaster. If you work in this kind
of office, don't just go with the flow. Instead, establish high personal standards for file organization and develop methods that
enable you to meet them. It's not easy to go against the prevailing culture of an organization, particularly when the
methods of communicating disapproval are subtle.
Nevertheless, good file maintenance habits are so critical to
your success as a lawyer that you need to establish your own
standards, even if others are unhappy about it.

Chapter 2

Technology:
Use It or Lose Out

Impact of technology
on the legal profession

You are starting your legal career in a time of profound technological change. Technology has radically altered the practice of law in the past two decades, and the transformation will continue to accelerate as we move into an exciting new future.

> ❝In the 21st century, all debates will resolve into debates about technology.❞
>
> — PAUL MCLAUGHLIN

Not surprisingly, the impact of technology will be very significant in the area of legal ethics and professionalism, and applying the established principles of legal ethics to ever-changing circumstances will be an ongoing challenge. However, technology will have an even greater impact on the way lawyers work. It has become absolutely clear that lawyers cannot continue to work the way they did in the past. Lawyers in all types and sizes of legal organizations have concluded that the old methods are inefficient and unprofitable, and are using cutting-edge technology to invent a new legal workscape.

> ❝If the information on the Internet is proportional to the galaxy, the knowledge is proportional to Earth and the wisdom, to an electron. ❞
>
> — PAUL MCLAUGHLIN

For the most part, lawyers and legal organizations are **mid-tech followers**. They are conservative and passive about technology: they want to be presented with proven technology that improves their efficiency and profitability with a minimum of effort on their part and are not interested in practicing on the bleeding edge. They are also painfully aware of the tremendous capital investment needed to keep up and are hesitant to put out the bucks

> Law office technology is changing so quickly that you need to keep running to stay still.

needed to move forward if their existing technology seems to be functioning adequately.

A senior partner working late was standing in front of the shredder looking perplexed. "Can you make this thing work?" he said to a young associate who happened by. "Sure," said the associate. He inserted the document and pressed the start button. As the document disappeared, the partner watched carefully. "Good," he said. "I'll need three copies of that."

Today's new lawyers are more technologically adept than their predecessors. Most of you don't have a problem with the idea that a lawyer should use a keyboard. You are comfortable doing research electronically. You should be aware, however, that there are many areas of legal technology you don't learn about at law school, so don't underestimate the technological sophistication of some of the lawyers who have been practicing for a while. You can learn a lot from them.

Technology in the law office

Hardware and operating systems. You'll find a very wide range of technology in law offices. Most have PCs running Pentium-level chips and some version of Microsoft Windows, although there are still a few MAC and DOS systems around. Almost all legal support staff have computers on their desks. Most lawyers now have computers on their desks, but it is unclear if they are used productively or are just expensive paperweights. Most legal organizations now use laser printers, although some use bubble-jets. Networking is widespread, as is access to on-line search and research services, the Internet, scanners and CDs for research. Voice recognition software is making significant inroads among users willing to put in the effort needed to make it work.

Word processing. In the area of word processing, the technology revolution is already very far along. With astonishing speed, we moved from the manual to the electric to the automatic to the electronic typewriter, then to the stand-alone word processor, and then to the computer-based word processor. For a while, we used dot matrix and daisywheel printers, but we have now moved on to bubble-jets and lasers.

The software advanced even more quickly than the hardware. Early word-processing programs were remarkable advances over what went before, but they look primitive when compared to today's versions.

> You don't have to choose between Microsoft® Word® and Corel® WordPerfect®, both of which are truly outstanding achievements of the human intellect. Use the one you prefer as your primary word processor but become familiar with both. As you move back and forth between programs, think functions (saving a file) rather than commands (click File then Save).

Document assembly. The document assembly revolution is just beginning, but it has the potential to bring about many fundamental changes in the way lawyers apply their knowledge, and may result in a radical restructuring of the legal profession's knowledge base. Document assembly allows a legal organization to achieve greater productivity, increased efficiency, better quality control and quicker error correction.

> **Document assembly:** a process for creating legal and other documents by drawing variable information from a database and merging it with standard forms; may involve decision-making and user input

In a document assembly system, the computer prompts the user to enter **variable information** into a database. It then "assembles" documents by merging the variable information into pre-existing standardized forms, or "templates." "Smart templates" interact with the user through dialog boxes. These templates also contain logical coding that enables the computer to make legally correct choices among optional clauses and documents.

> **Variable information:** information that is unique to a particular matter, such as the names and addresses of the parties to a standard form contract or the names of the testator and executor of a will

There are several types of document assembly software:

- Commercial programs for specific practice areas like real estate conveyancing, corporate law or wills
- Programs that legal organizations can use to automate the processes of creating data files, making their own precedents into templates and assembling documents
- Highly customized and specialized document assembly systems that lawyers and legal organizations have developed for their own practices, ranging from simple macros to extremely complicated and sophisticated programs

Financial information systems. Technology has totally transformed the processes that legal organizations use to keep track of financial information. After an initial period of skepticism, lawyers have come to rely on computers to maintain their financial information. It is now virtually a given that lawyers keep their time dockets, disbursements information, trust records and general ledger transactions on a computer. The computer produces statements of account, trust statements and other financial reports used to manage the organization.

There are many financial programs in use in legal organizations, with widely varying degrees of sophistication. They are relevant to the new lawyer because you are judged, at least in part, by the information they produce.

Even corporate and government lawyers find they have to pay attention to financial information, because more and more law departments are "billing" internal clients for legal services.

Client and file information. One of the basic "back-office" jobs in a law office is keeping track of basic information about clients (names, addresses, phone numbers, etc.) and about files. In the past, this information was usually recorded on index cards and in books, but it is now, for the most part, stored in computer databases.

> Conflict of interest lapses are one of the fastest growing malpractice problems. Familiarize yourself with your organization's conflict system and use it.

There are many ways you can use the **client information** stored in your organization's computer. For example, you can significantly reduce the time you spend looking for phone numbers by keeping a current client information printout close at hand. As you become busier, you can refine this printout to highlight your most frequently called clients. Even better, you can access the client information electronically. You can also use the client information database to track your efforts at keeping in touch with clients.

You can use the **file information** stored in the computer to monitor how many files you have opened or closed, how many you have open at any time, and the areas of law in which you receive the most work. You can also use this information to fend off unreasonable demands on your time (see Chapter 7, "Time Management").

Time information. Legal organizations keep two types of time information: calendars and To-Do lists.

Calendars keep track of deadlines and appointments. Lawyers frequently work under strict time limits, and missing a deadline can result in severe embarrassment, legal liability and discipline complaints. Some key deadlines that need to be recorded and monitored: limitation dates, closing dates, registration dates, renewal dates, option dates and court dates. Appointments also need to be recorded; a missed meeting usually does not result in legal liability, but if you are late too frequently, your reputation suffers.

If you need your calendar when you are out of the office, get two — a personal one to carry with you and a duplicate back at the office. In the past, a personal calendar was usually a book, but many lawyers are now using "palm-top" personal information managers that they electronically synchronize with the calendars in their office computers.

In a legal organization consisting of more than one lawyer, there should be a central calendar that consolidates all the dates and deadlines relevant to the organization's work. Most computerized calendar systems do this if the computers are networked.

A **To-Do list** tracks the work you need to do to meet your deadlines. It also monitors work that does not have firm deadlines—if you don't keep an eye on this kind of work, it can slip through the cracks and come back and bite you. You may, for instance, have thought that you could put off doing a will for another week, only to learn that the testator has died. An electronic To-Do list automatically rolls items forward until they are deleted and allows you to prioritize your work.

Several programs link the client, file and time information in one relational database. Some also link to financial and word-processing programs. The ultimate goal is an integrated information management system that makes all the information available whenever you need it.

Research. Legal research is another area where new technology has resulted in significant change, and the revolutionary wars are not over. Three contenders are still standing: free and not-so-free Internet sites that offer relatively raw legal information, direct access and Internet sites that offer value-added information, and CD ROMs. The next few years promise to be very interesting as these three vie for supremacy. No matter what, books are on their way out.

> Technological change in legal research has produced a new occupation: freelance legal researcher. For more information, see Chapter 11, "Planning Your Career".

Communication. Lawyers make their living by communicating, so it is not surprising that our profession has adopted many of the remarkable new communication technologies—fax, multi-function telephones, cell phones, internal and external e-mail, intranets, and the Internet. In the process, however, we have significantly sped up the pace of practice, generating new issues and concerns.

The use of the Internet has generated several ethical discussions. One controversy concerned whether lawyers could send e-mail without encrypting it. The first ethical opinions on this issue were all over the map, but a consensus now seems to have emerged that it is proper to send unencrypted e-mail when the client gives an informed consent. Particularly sensitive information, however, should be encrypted or, in some cases, not delivered by e-mail at all. A similar controversy arose with respect to cell phones, with the same basic result. The fundamental admonition is that you should seek your client's consent and use reasonable judgment based on the existing principles of our ethical codes when deciding whether it is appropriate to use a new communication medium.

Another ethical argument has arisen in relation to the use of the World Wide Web to advertise legal services. Most jurisdictions have taken a "hands-off" approach to this issue, although some have imposed very restrictive regulations, such as a requirement that all Internet advertisements require prior approval. No consensus has emerged, and this promises to be an interesting ongoing debate.

Litigation support. Lawyers are using new technology to help with trial prep and courtroom presentation.

Specialized database programs help in the management of cases involving a large number of documents. These programs allow for the documents to be coded and scanned for easy access. A few lawyers who have become experts on these programs have left active practice to become consultants to other lawyers, creating yet another new legal subspeciality.

There are also programs that index and annotate transcripts. Others analyze and organize all the information relevant to a lawsuit, such as facts, law, parties, witnesses, opposing counsel, experts, etc.

Video depositions and discoveries are now routine.

Technology has always played a role in the production of demonstrative evidence for use in court, and we are now witnessing a natural evolution in the use of computer-based animation and computer-generated models. Instead of bringing a skeleton into court, you can show the jury a striking computer-generated video clip that demonstrates vividly how the spine works, how the vertebrae fit together and what happened to your client's neck when her car was hit from behind. Lawyers also use high-tech whiteboards, document projectors and presentation programs in court.

How much technology is enough?

Most lawyers are interested in finding out how to use their computers more productively.

Cyberspace lawyers pursue a revolutionary high-tech vision. They buy the latest, fastest, most powerful hardware and software, push their systems to the limit, and use technology to continually improve their practices. They automate as much as they can so it is efficient for them to spend a lot of time at the keyboard. Their technology replaces support staff.

The cyberspace law office is a good business concept for a few lawyers but not for most. The danger for cyberspace lawyers is spending too much time programming and not enough actually practicing law.

> **Closure**
>
> Many lawyers like the way computers give them a quicker experience of closure. In the past they would dictate a document, wait for the draft, review the file, correct the draft, wait for the final, review the file, proofread the final and then send it out. They kept an enormous amount of pending work in their heads. Now they can complete a document in one sitting. The time involved is not much longer than the old way, once you factor in the correcting and proofreading time, and the real benefit is that the draft never goes into the pending work stream, so the lawyer experiences significantly less stress.

Most lawyers are **mid-tech.** They leave most of the keyboarding to their support staff but use their own computers when it is more productive. Some of the tasks mid-tech lawyers have found they can do efficiently are entering time dockets, time management, creating unique documents, case management, accessing client information, legal research and generating forms that require a minimum of inputting.

A misuse of technology

Sometimes, lawyers decide to start a law practice on a shoe-string. They don't have much in the way of cash reserves and can't hire support staff, so they do their own word processing with the intention of hiring someone to take it over when they generate enough cash flow. They may have fast, shiny new hardware and software, but they don't bother to put much effort into developing computer tools to make themselves more efficient because they hope their hands-on involvement with the computer will end shortly.

When they begin to attract work, they think they are busy because they work long hours, but in fact, they're just ineffi-cient. They soon find they don't make enough money to com-pensate themselves properly for the hours they put in, and they don't understand why they work so hard but take so little home. They often fail to recognize that most potential clients don't feel comfortable trusting their important legal matters to a lawyer who doesn't appear to be successful enough to afford support staff. These lawyers never seem to have time for the important entrepreneurial, organizational and marketing work that is needed to build a viable business, so their practices are weak and vulnerable. Some never arrive at that elusive day when they can hire someone to take over the clerical work.

Technology and the job interview

Here are 10 technology questions you can ask when

interviewing for a legal position:

1. What does your business plan say about technology? (You don't have one? Hmm.)
2. What will I be able to delegate to support staff and what will I be expected to do myself?
3. Will I have my own up-to-date computer? How often will it be upgraded?
4. Will I get a laptop if I have to travel? Will I have remote access when I am away from the office?
5. Will I be on a network?
6. Will I have access to the Internet? E-mail? My own e-mail account?
7. Will I have access to online legal research? CDs?
8. What word-processing software is used?
9. Do you use document assembly? How extensively?
10. What case management and financial information management software is used? What information will I have access to?

Push your phone to the limit

- Figure out how to use features like speed dialing and conferencing
- Use voice mail to leave messages
- Change your voice message every day
- Learn how to forward voice mails to your assistant with instructions on how to handle the call
- Link your phone into your computer so you can dial out from your personal information management software

Well, what should I do?

So, how should a new lawyer respond to this rapidly changing environment?

1. Embrace technological change. As the chapter title implies, if you don't embrace it, you will lose out.

2. Figure out the appropriate level of technology for you. Do you want to use proven technology to make you more efficient and profitable (mid-tech) or do you want to be a trailblazer (high-tech)?

3. Recognize that both mid-tech and high-tech are moving targets, so you will have to keep moving forward just to stay still.

4. Keep yourself informed. Mainstream computer books and magazines do not address the specific needs of the legal profession. For that information, you need to tap into specialty literature, such as the books, magazines and newsletters published by the Law Practice Management Section of the American Bar Association (http://www.abanet.org/lpm) and James Publishing (http://www.lawofficecomputing.com). You can also access good information over the Internet by subscribing to legal technology lists and visiting the web sites of law practice management consultants and legal software suppliers.

5. Jump in. Given the speed of technological change, it
   is tempting to wait until the next generation of hardware or software becomes available. The problem is,
   as soon as the next generation arrives, the one after
   that comes over the horizon and tempts you to wait
   again. In the meantime, you lag further and further
   behind. It's not hard to move from one software version to the next, but jumping over several versions at
   one time can be very stressful.

Technology is penetrating all aspects of the practice of law. It
is revolutionizing the way we work—from how we produce
documents to how we organize our time to how we present
evidence in court. An exciting new world is coming into existence. Be part of it!

Chapter 3

Let's Get Personal about Practice Management

As a lawyer, you make innumerable decisions in the course of managing your practice. Some are trivial, but many have a profound impact on your clients, your assistants, the organization in which you work and your own life.

Personal practice management deals with how you manage your own practice. It is concerned with questions like, *how do you organize your work? how do you keep your clients informed? how do you keep your files organized?* Anything that helps you make better personal practice management decisions helps your career.

You can dramatically improve the quality of your personal practice management decision-making by being organized about it. There are many models for decision-making to select from, and you should choose one that works best for you.

If you don't already use a decision-making paradigm, try the one outlined below.

Eight steps to better personal practice management decisions

Eight steps are involved in making personal practice management decisions:

1. Write down the problem clearly

> **❝**A [management] decision is a judgment. It is a choice between alternatives. It is rarely a choice between right and wrong. It is at best a choice between 'almost right' and 'probably wrong' — but much more often a choice between two courses of action neither of which is provably more nearly right than the other.**❞**
>
> — PETER DRUCKER, *The Effective Executive*

Personal practice management focuses on the individual lawyer.

Law firm management focuses on the organization.

2. Identify your personal characteristics that may contribute to the problem or block solutions

3. Identify your personal characteristics that may contribute to solutions

4. Identify circumstances in your environment that may contribute to the problem or block solutions

5. Identify circumstances in your environment that may enable solutions

6. Imagine, as concretely as you can, what it will be like to have the problem solved

7. Create one or more solutions (procedures, personal policies, rules, routines, habits) to deal with the problem on an ongoing basis

8. Review your solutions and make changes as necessary

Although the process is laid out as a series of steps, you don't have to go through them in order. The goal is to give yourself as much information as possible so you make the best decision under the circumstances. Step 1 may be near the end of the process because you may not really know what the problem is until you have worked on it for a while. However, make sure you work on **all** of the first six steps before you move to Step 7.

The purpose of **Step 1** is to discipline you to clarify the problem before you start looking for solutions. When you put the problem in writing, you should address some basic questions: Why is it a problem? Whose problem is it? How important is it to find a solution?

Steps 2 and 3 encourage you to take a journey inside yourself. What is it about you that makes this a problem? Is it more of a problem for you than for others? If so, why? What personal characteristics do you have that can contribute to solutions? It is important to be objective when answering these questions.

Steps 4 and 5 require you to look around and gather as much information as you can. In other words, you have to research the problem and potential solutions. What is there in your environment that may be making the problem worse or blocking solutions? What is there that could contribute to solutions? Is there a technological solution? Is the right technology available? Are there people who can help? Is money an issue? Are other resources available or missing? What have others done to solve the problem?

> Involve your assistants in solving your personal practice management problems, especially when the problems and solutions have a direct impact on them.

At this point, you might want to involve others in the process, such as your assistant or another lawyer who seems to have solved the problem. In fact, you may want to convert the process into a group decision-making process.

Before you can create a better future for yourself in reality, you must first create it in your mind. **Step 6** asks you to think into the future and imagine what it will be like to have licked the problem. Try to envision the reality you want to create. Imagine how you will feel and how others will react to the changes you are contemplating. How will you react to their reactions? Think about both the upsides and the downsides of solutions.

In **Step 7,** you choose one or more solutions. This is where many people want to start: as soon as they have identified a problem, they crave a solution that deals with the immediate crisis. As a consequence, they make poor, short-sighted decisions when they should be looking for long-term solutions that deal with the problem on an ongoing basis.

Be careful not to get stuck because you can't find the perfect solution. It doesn't exist! Reread the quotation from Peter Drucker at the beginning of this chapter: there are no "correct" answers to your personal practice management problems. You are embarking on a long-term, experimental process during which you try many things until you find what works for you.

Step 8 is the reason for writing all the decision-making information down. Developing good personal practice management skills may require you to address some bad work habits that may be very deeply entrenched. Undoing them will take time, patience and determination, and you should expect to backslide a few times before new habits become established. So set a date for a review. Your first review should take place in three months, with follow-ups at six months and one year. When you do the reviews, refer back to your notes to remind yourself what went into your original decisions.

An example

Here is an example of the decision process in action:

1. **Write the problem down clearly**
   I need to get better at returning clients' phone calls. I haven't lost any clients yet, but it is just a matter of time. I am embarrassed by my bad habits in this area and I am concerned that the partners are starting to notice. It is unfair of me to expect my assistant to cover for me any more.

2. **Identify your personal characteristics that may contribute to the problem**

   When I get very focused on a legal problem, I neglect my phone messages because I find the phone very intrusive. Then I make the problem worse by ignoring the second and third messages because I am embarrassed. When it gets really bad, I get my assistant to call, which makes a bad situation worse for everyone. I return calls to people I like first, and sometimes don't get to the others.

3. **Identify your personal characteristics that may contribute to solutions**

   I really like my clients and want to do a good job for them. I am basically pretty self-disciplined and I am committed to being an organized lawyer.

4. **Identify circumstances in the environment that may contribute to the problem or block solutions**

   The firm does not set a high standard in this area; some partners are notorious for neglecting their phone messages; I will have to do this on my own. The receptionist's desk is a long way from my office so I don't receive new messages as soon as I should, and we don't use e-mail for phone messages.

5. **Identify circumstances in the environment that may enable solutions**

   Both the receptionist and my assistant are willing to help me with this problem. We have very good phone & internal e-mail systems.

6. Imagine, as concretely as you can, what it will be like to have solved the problem

I will not have the anxiety of a huge accumulation of unreturned phone messages. I will not have angry clients. I will develop a reputation for being accessible and responsive, which will attract more clients. The partners will be happy they hired me. My assistant will be happier. I will sleep better at night as I achieve success. If I backslide, I will be worse off than if I don't start because I will have created expectations I don't follow through with.

7. Create one or more solutions (procedures, personal policies, rules, routines, habits) to deal with the problem on an ongoing basis

Phone call return policies:

1. *I will set aside certain times of day for file work and other times for returning phone calls. I will confine work that requires heavy concentration to file work times and keep the phone call times for phone calls and light reading. I will let my clients know that they should not expect to be able to contact me during my file work times unless their call is truly urgent, but that they can expect me to call them back right away if they call during the phone call times.*

2. *Except for truly urgent calls, I will return phone calls in the order in which they came in.*

3. *I will not ask my assistant to return stale messages.*

4. *I will ask my assistant to handle as many routine calls as possible.*

5. *When I am not taking calls, I will tell the receptionist when I will be available again so clients can be told when to expect a return call.*

6. *When an urgent call comes in and both my assistant and I are unavailable, the receptionist will e-mail both of us informing us of the call.*

7. *I will overcome my reluctance to leave long voice-mail messages if it is clear that the client prefers this method of communication.*

8. *When I promise to return a call by a certain time, I will keep that promise 100% of the time.*

8. Review the problem and your solution and make changes as necessary

Review set for _____.

Well, what should I do?

Here are a dozen personal practice management projects for you to consider. The first eight of these projects are applicable to any legal setting; the last four are more specifically directed at private practice lawyers:

1. Handling incoming and outgoing mail efficiently
2. Keeping my personal calendar synchronized with my assistant's calendar
3. Improving my response time on work that my assistant has completed
4. Cleaning off my desk at the end of each day
5. Arriving at court, appointments and meetings early
6. Keeping my clients informed

7. Ensuring the accuracy of every document that goes out with my name

8. Remembering to recognize important events in my assistant's life

> As you read this book, look for other projects you can add to the list.

9. Contacting at least one potential new client every week

10. Posting my time dockets immediately

11. Keeping track of my billings

12. Discussing fees and disbursements with every new client

Review the list of projects and rank them according to your own priorities. Start working on the most important project using the process outlined above. At the beginning of each month for the next year, start another personal practice management project.

Chapter 4

Working with
Your Assistant

Your first job as a lawyer may mark the first time you have somebody working for you. Although it's an exciting and important step in your development, it can be quite scary because suddenly you are responsible for another person's psychological and economic well-being. It can be particularly difficult if your assistant is older and more experienced than you, or has an intimidating personality, especially if you don't have any supervisory experience.

And, of course, you didn't take any courses in law school to prepare you for this very significant responsibility.

Being a leader does not mean being a dictator

Your position as the lawyer in the hierarchical lawyer-assistant relationship has thrust you into leadership. Ideally, you and your assistant can develop a working relationship in which she or he feels strongly motivated to work hard for you. But you are the boss, so the major responsibility for fostering a good working arrangement falls on your shoulders.

You lead by **setting a good example**, by applying the same standards to yourself that you expect from your assistant. If you want your assistant to be hard-working and professional, you have to be hard-working and professional. If you want

❝ Employees want to have opportunities to learn and grow on the job, to use a variety of skills, to be recognized for their accomplishments. Every employee wants to be shown dignity and respect and wants to participate in decisions that affect him or her on the job. They want to understand the big picture and how their work contributes both to the needs of the firm and to the needs of the client. **❞**

— ANN E. KRUSE,
"Getting Top Value for your Payroll Dollar", *Law Practise Management*, April 1993, 54

❝You cannot bully an employee to excellence. **❞**

— PAT YEVICS

❝No matter how good a lawyer you are, you can be no better than the people around you. If you hire hard-working, motivated people and treat them well, they will stay with you and help you build your practice. **❞**

— K. WILLIAM GIBSON, *How to Build and Manage a Personal Injury Practice*

Assistant: as used in this book, a person who works for a lawyer

If your work is not getting done on time, it doesn't necessarily follow that your assistant is not working hard enough. Other explanations include:

• Understaffing
• Lack of appropriate technological resources
• Inefficient procedures
• Insufficient training

your assistant to care about clients, you'll have to show that you care. If you want sacrifice, you'll have to sacrifice.

You also lead by **communicating**.

Communicating your goals. Your assistant makes numerous day-to-day decisions in the administration of your practice. If you take the time to communicate your goals clearly, he or she knows what you want without having to refer every detail back to you. And be careful not to send conflicting messages. If you want to encourage independent decision-making, don't criticize sarcastically every time a mistake is made, or you will encourage the opposite of the very behavior you want to promote.

Communicating your instructions. You should learn to communicate your instructions clearly. When you say, "Please see if John Smith can come in for a meeting", do you mean, "Find out when the client is available; I will decide on the time for the meeting"? Or do you mean, "Arrange the meeting, send a confirming letter and put the time and date in my calendar"? Clarifying your expectations takes time, particularly at the beginning of your relationship, but it pays big dividends. Eventually, you and your assistant will work together like doubles tennis champions, each with a deep intuitive understanding of the other's moves.

Communicating approval and disapproval. You also have to learn how to communicate approval and disapproval. In the long run, approval is a more powerful motivator, but many lawyers seem to believe that it is a sign of weakness to compliment an assistant for a good performance. After all, they seem to think, the assistant knows I would say something if things weren't going well, so it should be obvious from the fact I haven't said anything that I'm happy with the way the job is being done. To most employees, however, silence implies disapproval or criticism and can be very **de**motivating.

> Lawyers who don't express approval when it is deserved abrogate their leadership responsibilities and neglect an important motivator of excellence.

Everyone is different; you need to use rewards that work for your assistant, even if they don't make sense to you. Analyze your assistant's value system to figure out how to encourage the work habits and quality standards you want.

If you find yourself working long hours, the problem may be that you are not delegating effectively. Learn not to micro-manage. Establish procedures that allow your assistant to handle assignments with minimal instructions. For instance:

• Instead of dictating a letter to follow up on a court order sent to another lawyer for approval, create a standard letter and dictate, "Please follow up on the Smith order". Better still, have your assistant automatically follow up within a pre-set time.

• Train your assistant to set up routine events (appointments, meetings, closings, discoveries, motion dates, etc.), including automatically sending out standard confirming letters.

Supervision, evaluation and trust

Supervision is a relatively unstructured, day-to-day interaction between you and your assistant in which you respond to your assistant's handling of the work you assign.

The short-term purpose of supervision is to make sure the work has been done correctly. From a longer-term perspective, however, the goal of supervision is to motivate your assistant to work hard and well when you're not present. In the best lawyer-assistant relationships, the assistant works independently and refers back to the lawyer only when the need arises. To develop a relationship in which you can delegate almost complete responsibility for the detailed processing of your work, you need an assistant you can trust.

> Nothing kills productivity faster than lack of trust. Are you trustworthy?

Perhaps less obviously, your assistant has to trust you as well. There are risks involved in taking initiative, the biggest being the threat of disapproval. Your assistant's willingness to accept the risks depends, at least in part, on the self-confidence she or he develops as you work together. That self-confidence depends, in turn, on the degree to which you can be trusted to assume your responsibility as the employer not to delegate work that is beyond your assistant's ability. Challenges are appropriate, but throwing your assistant into the deep end without a life jacket is not.

Evaluation is the more formal personnel development process designed to provide periodic structured performance feedback. Your organization probably has a set schedule and format for evaluations, so you won't be entirely on your own.

Evaluation also requires trust. It is a very personal process in which we have to reveal critical thoughts about others that we would probably be just as happy to keep to ourselves. It also exposes us to another person's potentially critical opinions. In many organizations, the negativity that is associated with evaluation has resulted in the process becoming little more than a charade. That is a pity, because a performance evaluation can be an important bonding experience in which the lawyer and assistant lay the foundations for strong teamwork based on shared goals and clear communication.

Here are some pointers to help you with the evaluation process:

- Plan for the evaluation; use a performance evaluation form and think about it ahead of time
- Evaluate the performance, not the performer
- Focus on strengths, not weaknesses or pathology ("We need to work on increasing your output," not "You don't work hard enough" or "You're lazy")
- Focus on the future, not the past
- Let your assistant participate in the evaluation; don't let it become a one-way communication with you doing all the talking
- Reinforce your assistant's importance to you, the organization in which you both work and the clients
- Work together to set a limited number of achievable, mutually acceptable goals, record them and work together toward their achievement
- Ask what you can do differently to help your assistant become more effective
- Be fair

What Not to Do

Experts tell us that the main reason for the high turnover among legal assistants is not the money but the shabby treatment they get from the lawyers for whom they work. Lawyers often treat their assistants with disgraceful and unprofessional discourtesy. They come across as superior, pompous, callous and uncouth. Here is what not to do to your assistant:

Memo

To: Joe You-think-you're so-smart Lawyer
From: Sandy Your-about-to-be-ex Legal Assistant

I'm out of here. You are the worst boss I have ever had. Good luck finding someone else who is willing to put up with your abuse.

I do have to thank you for one thing: you taught me everything a boss should not be. In case you're interested, here is how I see our not-so-wonderful time together.

21 Rules for Winning the Boss-from-Hell Sweepstakes

1. Always give me a new pile of work just before quitting time. An adrenaline rush is refreshing at that time of day and besides, why waste the night sleeping when I can be up worrying?

2. When you assign a rush job, interrupt me every 10 minutes to check how it is going. Better still, hover over me and tense up every time I make a typo. See how much it improves my accuracy.

3. When you give me several jobs to do, don't tell me which has priority. I'm psychic, you know.

4. Don't tell me about any special instructions for a job until it is done, so you can make me feel stupid for not guessing them. What the heck, I don't mind doing the work again.

5. Be sure to remind me about a long-term project like sorting out my hard drive right after you have given me enough work to keep me going flat out for three weeks. (What am I saying? I can use my weekends to sort out my hard drive! Who needs recovery time? Sorry.)

6. Never tell me where you are going when you leave the office. I appreciate the chance to exercise my creativity when someone asks where you are.

7. Make me work late as often as you like. I don't have a life beyond work. Like you, I adore this place and really have nothing else to do.

8. Never introduce me to your clients. I have no right to know who they are. In the food chain here, I am plankton. Besides, it's fun to try to figure out who they are when you refer to them later.

9. Always remember: your lack of organization is my problem.

10. If I do a good job, please take all the credit. If it gets out that I made a contribution around here,

someone might accidentally pay me a compliment, which would delay me from reaching my goal of flushing the last remnants of my self-esteem down the toilet.

11. If anything goes wrong, please make sure I get all the blame, but tell everyone except me. I like it when people talk about me, and there are plenty of folks around here who are glad to let me know when you are unhappy. A bonus: all your whining puts you out front in the martyr of the year contest.

12. Wait until my performance review to tell me what my goals should have been. It's more fun that way.

13. Expect me to care about what happens in your files, but treat me like a mushroom unless you have something to brag or complain about.

14. Don't let me take any training courses because I'm not the least bit interested in improving myself. Besides, I'd probably just use my new skills to get a better job. Better I should remain untrained and stay here working for you.

15. Here are a bunch of personal behaviors that just make me want to cuddle you, you big old teddy bear. Don't refer to me by my name. Don't open a door for me, even if my arms are full. When you need something, holler at me from your office so everyone can hear. Make me get you coffee but never get coffee for me. Pull me out of my break to send a one-page fax you could have sent yourself. Use hand gestures to signal me to come and go. Wink at others when you are talking to me. Eat, slurp coffee, belch, cough, sneeze and sniff into the dictation machine. Lie.

16. Never say "Please" or "Thank you". Why should you? I get paid to do what I'm told.

17. Don't fight for me at raise time. After all, I'm not here for the money, even if you are.

18. Tell me about all your little personal problems. I don't have any of my own, so it's interesting to hear yours. I find it so hard to believe that your spouse doesn't understand you. And I especially liked your complaint about all the tax you had to pay on your bonus. I don't have any tax problems. Then again, I didn't get a bonus either.

19. Tell me what you really think about the clients and this organization. It helps me keep my equilibrium when I know that the whole point of this operation is to make as much money as possible off a bunch of hopeless boobs who don't even know what their legal rights are.

20. Include me in all your little conspiracies. It makes every day like a spy movie.

21. Don't let me develop any hopes or goals of my own. My only ambition is to support you and your goals, even if you are a shallow, self-serving, sycophantic, materialistic workaholic who is completely bereft of the slightest scintilla of human decency.

The Staff Policy Manual

Most organizations have a Staff Policy Manual that outlines their organization's position on a wide variety of employer-employee issues. In your dealings with your assistant, you are expected to comply with and enforce the policies in the manual, so you should maintain a current copy and refer to it when needed.

Well, what should I do?

Here are two more tips for improving your working relationship with your assistant:

- Never underestimate the power of positive expectations, participation, civility and recognition

- Prevent a build-up of tensions by giving your assistant a chance to vent from time to time; at least once a month, sit down and ask how things are going, then shut up and listen

Chapter 5

Communicating with Your Clients

Client service paradigm

Until recently, the **professional elite** paradigm shaped the thinking of the legal profession in North America. According to this model, lawyers were supposed to wait in their offices until the client came to them with a problem. They took charge of the problem, redefined it in legal terms and applied their specialized knowledge to come up with and implement a solution. They then billed their clients for what they (the lawyers) thought the work was worth and expected the clients to pay gratefully. Most clients accepted that they could not really understand what their lawyers did.

In the last couple of decades, social and economic forces like consumerism, competition, advertising, diversity and technology have undermined the professional elite approach, and it is now being replaced by the **client service** paradigm.

According to the new model, clients are no longer viewed as passive recipients of legal services—they are seen as consumers who participate actively in defining their legal problems and implementing solutions. The clients are in charge, and lawyers are now expected, subject to ethics, to act according to their instructions. Lawyers are teachers, sharing their legal knowledge with clients so they receive proper instructions. The value of legal services is not determined unilaterally by lawyers, but negotiated in a complex interaction between lawyers and clients.

> **❝**The key to delivering legal services in a way that ensures client cooperation and satisfaction is communication—communication that supports and enhances the client's value to you in a way that the client clearly sees and understands.**❞**
>
> —NOELLE C. NELSON, *Connecting with Your Client*

> **❝**Clients are not always right—the trick is to tell them that and keep them as clients.**❞**
>
> —based on a comment by JAMES MUSGROVE, *Excelling at Articles*

In this new era, the ability to communicate with clients is more important than ever. In the private sector, clients expect their lawyers to have excellent communication skills, and

> Client communication is now a survival issue.

they are ready to move on to another lawyer if they are disappointed. In the corporate, government and non-profit sectors, employers expect their lawyers to be active participants in projects, not just privileged advisers, and to be able to communicate with other project participants, such as scientists, engineers, financial and accounting experts.

Lawyers as communicators

Of course, most lawyers have always considered themselves to be excellent communicators. Lawyers trade in communication because legal services are almost invariably delivered through some form of written or oral communication. Indeed, without clear, concise lawyerly communication, there would be no law.

However, the revolution in client-lawyer relations has forced lawyers to realize that communication is more complex than they thought. They tend to be better at communicating their ideas than at listening, and they frequently miss many of the important emotional overtones in their communication, particularly with clients.

Content: what a
communication says

Content and form in client communication

Form: what a communication
looks and/or sounds like

Lawyers are usually very good about the **content** of their communications: they do not question the importance of truth, accuracy and completeness. Sometimes, however, they neglect the **form** of the communication, which, from the client's point of view, is often just as important. For example, they may ask a client to sign a document littered with strikeouts and amendments because it has the same legal effect as a clean document, failing to take into consideration the negative impression it produces in anyone who sees it.

Here are some form questions to apply to your documents:

• Are they functionally laid out?
• Do you use tables of contents and headings to help readers find their way around?
• Do they look good? Do you use a variety of clear, pleasing fonts? Do your printer and copier produce clear, crisp images? Do you use document covers?
• Are the spelling and grammar perfect?
• Do you use plain, clear language?

Levels of formality

Internal communications take place within an organization between and among lawyers and support staff. They are usually informal, particularly in organizations where people know each other well. They often contain confidential information and elliptical personal observations which may be misinterpreted. It is therefore important for law firm insiders to be careful not to inadvertently communicate in an inappropriately informal manner when they are in the presence of clients or outsiders.

Client communications occupy a middle ground between internal communications and communications with others outside the organization. They should be more formal than internal communications, but at times may be less formal than communications with other outsiders, depending on the client. When you find the right balance, your clients feel they have a special relationship with you and your firm that combines an appropriate level of intimacy and respect.

Instrumental and affective dimensions of client communications

Instrumental: what does the communication accomplish (does it make a point, inform, present an argument, counter a position, put forward a question, advance a negotiation, etc.)?

Every communication has two dimensions—the **instrumental** and the **affective**.

Lawyers tend to focus on the instrumental dimensions of their communications. They try to express themselves as clearly and, often, as unemotionally as possible. However, every communication has an emotional, or affective, impact on its recipient. A negative emotional reaction in the recipient of a communication can impair or even destroy its instrumental intent.

Affective: what feelings does the communication produce?

Consider the following statement by a lawyer to a client:

"Your divorce is likely to cost you $10,000."

The instrumental purpose of the communication is to convey a prediction of what it will cost to complete the divorce.

The affective impact of the statement depends on the state of mind of the client. To one client, the statement might be a devastating blow because it means the divorce is unaffordable.

To the next, it might be depressing but acceptable. To the third, who thought the divorce was going to cost three times that much, it is a relief.

If you ignore the affective dimension of communication, you miss more than half of what is going on, and this can lead to serious unintended results. In the above example, you could deliver your message calmly, straightforwardly and objectively, but although you intend to be supportive and informative, your words might come across as cold and brutal to your client.

The lesson, then, is to always monitor the affective dimension in your client communications.

> Experts say that only a small proportion of a person's decision to believe in or trust another hinges on the communicator's words or content. The decision depends mostly on voice tone and body language. Auditory resonances and intonation count for most of our emotional influence, believability and trust when people hear us but cannot see us, such as when we are on the telephone.

The three affective goals for every client communication

Your goal in every client communication should be to create a client who feels:

> "I am **heard** here."
> "I am **cared for** here."
> "I am **safe** here."

I am *heard* here. Lawyers are great at talking, but they aren't always so good at listening. Here are some ways to be attentive so your clients feel "heard":

DO

- Use open-ended questions to encourage your client to talk
- Paraphrase your clients' comments to make sure you understand what they are trying to communicate
- Use encouraging gestures and words
- Be still—don't fidget, play with paper clips, shuffle paper, squirm in your chair, pace, gaze out the window, glance at your watch, etc.
- Provide closure: at the end of the meeting, review it, set goals and deadlines, and invite questions
- Send your client a copy of your memo to file summarizing the meeting

DO NOT

- Try to listen while you are reading documents; either put the papers aside and read them later, or ask your client to wait while you glance through them
- Try to take notes while you are listening; either go through the information twice, once to listen and once to take notes, or train yourself to keep brief outline notes during meetings and then dictate a detailed memorandum from your notes immediately afterward
- Permit interruptions unless your client has been warned in advance
- Interrupt or digress
- Cross-examine clients who haven't been warned that you are preparing them for being cross-examined

Encouraging words:
- Yes.
- Uh-huh.
- I see.
- And then ...
- Okay.
- What happened next?

I am *cared* for here. Your goal here is to communicate to your client that you understand that:

• Their legal problems have non-legal dimensions
• Your legal solutions have non-legal consequences
• There are emotional overtones to the facts they present
• Their feelings may be more important to them than the facts

You relate to your clients' feelings through **empathy**. You don't necessarily experience the same feelings as they do, but you acknowledge the existence of their emotions and their right to feel the way they do.

Clients may well be experiencing many intense negative emotions when they meet with you, such as:

• **Fear** of lawyers, legal procedures, the unknown, "the system", having to speak in public, conflict, confrontation, being taken advantage of, action, retaliation
• **Anxiety at the prospect of loss** of liberty, reputation, privacy, relationship with a loved one, status, privilege, money, property, children, friends, control
• **Vulnerability**
• **Anger and bitterness**, particularly if they see themselves as victims

---

Pop Quiz

Your client says, "My husband committed adultery after 30 years of marriage." The empathetic response is:

a) "Oh, good, that means we have grounds for an immediate divorce."

b) "All men are alike. I'll make sure the S.O.B. pays for this."

c) "You must really feel betrayed."

The behaviors you are likely to see in clients in the grip of strong feelings include:

- Avoidance and denial
- Hostile confrontation
- Lying, fantasy and selective memory
- Emotional manipulation
- Even attempts at seduction

Although you should relate to your clients with empathy, it doesn't follow that you should lose your professional objectivity or become a patsy to every emotional plea that a client may throw at you. Watch out for clients who are:

- Users
- Chronic complainers
- Compulsive negotiators
- People who want to transfer all responsibility for their problems to you
- People who confuse attention with affection
- People whose real problem is that they need attention
- People who are buying human contact

One way to establish empathy with a client is to use client-appropriate language. Don't talk down to your clients; instead, mold your communication to their needs. Use vocabulary your clients can understand. In particular, avoid legalese and jargon. Modify the tone, volume, pace and expressiveness of your communications to suit the situation.

You can also establish empathy by using active listening techniques, such as open questions, encouragement and reflections on the emotional content of their communications.

I am *safe* here. Your clients feel safe if they are confident that you are in control. You show that you are in control by the way you manage:

> Clients who feel safe move from vulnerable to self-confident, from defensive to ready for action, and from anxious to comfortable. They are also more willing to pay their legal bills.

- The legal problem
- Your time, your space and the file
- Your relationship with your client
- Financial arrangements
- Your emotions
- Your ego

You can show you are in control of the **legal problem** if you:

- Stay focused on the issues and don't get diverted by red herrings
- Document your progress
- Conscientiously keep your client informed
- Plan ahead
- Visibly stand up for your client's rights and are not intimidated by other lawyers or judges

You show you are in control of your **time, space and the file** if you:

- Arrive at meetings, appointments, discoveries and court hearings on time
- Make sure there are no other files visible when you meet with your clients (clients who see other clients' files wonder if other clients see their files)

- Meet your clients in rooms that are comfortable and conducive to confidential communication
- Keep your files organized (see Chapter 1, "How to Make Friends with Your Files")

You stay in control of **the relationship with your client** if you:

- Stay calm
- Listen
- Convey quiet confidence and visible competence
- Always act ethically
- Refuse to argue with your client
- Encourage your assistant to develop good relationships with your clients

If a client becomes hostile or confrontational, try this: "I understand that you are upset, but it doesn't help us deal with the problem when you take your frustration out on me. If you have any doubt that I'm on your side–if you think for any reason that I'm part of the problem and not part of the solution–then maybe you should have a different lawyer."

Pause and give the client a chance to respond.

If the response is appropriate, say, "Okay let's get back to our discussion." Otherwise, terminate the meeting, and if necessary, the relationship.

You manage the **financial arrangements** if you:

- Discuss the basis on which fees and disbursements are charged and expectations about payment, and, if you can, give an estimate of the likely cost at the **first** interview
- Put the fee discussions and payment expectations in writing
- Get an advance against fees and disbursements (a retainer) when one is appropriate (check your local ethical rules)

- Bill regularly
- If subsequent developments make your initial estimate unreasonably low, bring your client in for a further discussion of the fees and give your client a chance to decide whether to proceed, pull out or find another way to resolve the problem
- Phone the client in advance if a bill is going to be larger than you anticipated
- Be reasonable when incurring disbursements
- Follow up quickly if a bill is not paid on time

You manage your **emotions** by staying objective (See Chapter 12, "Balancing the Law and Your Life").

Finally, you manage your **ego** if you simply remember that the file is the client's, not yours; the problem is your client's, not yours; and the needs that are to be served are the client's, not yours.

Well, what should I do?

Read *Through the Clients' Eyes: New Approaches to Get Clients to Hire You Again and Again* by Henry W. Ewalt (ABA, 1994). It will change the way you practice. I guarantee it.

Chapter 6

Money Matters

Many new lawyers find legal practice distressingly mercenary. They quickly learn that their commitment to justice, fairness and equality must always be tempered by concerns about money.

Regardless of the kind of legal organization you work in, money matters, so let's talk about it.

Your expectations

Most of you became lawyers for idealistic reasons. You assumed your work would generate a good income, but you probably didn't have a clear understanding of how that would happen. At law school, you received conflicting messages about money from many sources: teachers, fellow students, just about everyone who knew you were studying law and the media, including:

> **❝**Profit . . . is the *result* of doing things right rather than the purpose of business activity. . . . Profitability is a measurement of how well the business discharges its functions in serving market and customer. Above all, it is a restraint; unless profit is adequate to cover the risks, a [business] will not be able to attain its objectives.**❞**
>
> — PETER DRUCKER, *Management: Tasks, Responsibilities, Practices*

- "Law is a noble calling, and lawyers who are concerned about money are vulgar, crass and ignoble."
- "We teach the law as an academic professional discipline, and how you make a living from it is beneath our concern (although we don't teach for nothing)."
- "Rich, successful lawyers are poor role models."
- "Law is about protecting your clients' property interests, not increasing your own."

> I still remember the first time I had to say to a worthy client with a worthy case, "I can't help you because you don't have enough money." I sugar-coated it, but that's what I meant.

• "Private practice is full of greedy lawyers."
• "Law is about making money."
• "Rich, successful lawyers are admirable role models."
• "You'll have it made when you become a lawyer, with lots of money and plenty of material possessions."

All these messages are partly true and partly false, and it's no wonder new lawyers are confused about the role of money in their chosen profession.

Where does the money to pay me come from?

If you are independently wealthy and don't need to worry about money, you can skip the next section.

> To survive, a legal organization must supply legal services that the sources of its revenues perceive to be valuable.

If you're still reading, you are among the vast majority of lawyers who expect to earn their living from client fees or to be compensated by the legal organization in which they work. No legal organization can survive without a steady flow of cash to pay its lawyers. Money paid to lawyers—professional compensation—is the largest single category of payments in a legal organization. So one question you need to ask is, where do legal organizations get their money? It depends on the type of organization:

• In private law firms, the money comes from the clients who purchase legal services
• In corporate law departments, it comes from the revenues generated by other departments, which in turn comes from the corporation's customers

- In government law departments, the ultimate source is tax revenues
- In nonprofit organizations, the money comes from endowments, grants and donations

The source of an organization's money shapes its expectations of its lawyers. In private practice, you'll have to deal with billings, collections, and profitability. In a corporate law department, your employer expects you to contribute, albeit indirectly, to corporate profitability. In government and nonprofit practices, you are expected to pay attention to the appropriateness of expenditures because you are a quasi-fiduciary of money that has been allocated for specified purposes.

But why should you, a new lawyer, be concerned about where the organization's money comes from? Aren't you better off to just practice law and let the organization worry about ensuring there is enough money to pay for everything? The answer depends on whether you want a future with the organization. If you don't, it doesn't matter. But if you do, you will eventually have to generate enough valuable services that can be converted into money to justify keeping you on as part of the organization. The sooner you learn how to focus your work so it contributes to the organization's cash flow, the more solid your future will be.

Money and professionalism

Sometimes ethical principles clash with money concerns. These clashes can happen in any type of practice. In private practice, you may experience tension between the pressure to

Cha-Ching!

bill and the obligation to turn down a file for which you are not yet competent. In corporate practice, you may be pressured to sign a financing document that is not 100% true. In government or nonprofit practice, you may be tempted to use resources inappropriately.

All lawyers have to work their way through the money issue. Most gradually come to accept its central importance in legal practice. However, if you find the continual focus on money personally offensive, you won't do anyone any good if you simply become bitter and angry about it. You can look for a firm or a corporate, government or nonprofit law department that is less fixated on money (that is, one that better matches your personal values). You can move out of practice into teaching, legal research or some other law-related occupation. You can leave the profession—law isn't for everyone. See Chapter 11, "Planning Your Career", for some career planning ideas.

A crusty old lawyer hired a recent graduate to help out with his practice. When he handed his young associate his first pay, he said, "I want you to understand two things about money and law. First, making money is the most important thing about practicing law… until you have enough."

He paused.

"Second, how much money is enough for you will be a measure of your character as a lawyer."

He paused again to let his comments sink in.

"For some lawyers, there is never enough. They are a disgrace to our profession. Others don't make enough to support themselves and their families. They lack judgment and should be doing something else. I hope you end up somewhere in the middle."

Pro bono

The opportunity to work pro bono is important for many new lawyers, and most legal organizations are willing to support a reasonable amount of unpaid work.

Pro bono client: a client who receives legal services for free or at a reduced fee

Some pro bono services are justified on ethical grounds: assisting people who don't have enough money to be able to access legal services is a professional obligation. Some may be justified on personal grounds: doing a case pro bono may be an opportunity to learn new law, develop new skills, promote a personal cause or help people you care about. These are laudable reasons for working for nothing and should be supported.

In private practice, pro bono work sometimes results from poor judgment about a client's willingness or ability to pay. When you learn that you are unlikely to be paid, you continue to work in the hope that something will work out instead of confronting the client. You don't advise the firm that you misjudged the situation. In effect, you let the client choose you as a personal charity. Of course, this is a poor way for a lawyer to take on pro bono work, but it's surprisingly common.

There is an infinite demand for free legal services. Since the need can never completely be met, you should establish selection criteria to guide your decisions on pro bono files.

Be careful not to let your pro bono work get out of hand. Unless you work in a legal services organization that is funded to do nothing but pro bono work, it can never be more than a secondary interest. Pro bono work may be free to the client, but it isn't free to you or your organization. Rent and other fixed overheads continue to run; the staff has to be paid; disbursements must be financed; and the

The same competence standards apply to pro bono work. You can't cut corners just because you aren't getting paid.

time you spend on your pro bono files is lost as billing time on other work. Too many large, interesting, demanding pro bono cases can sink a lawyer's career. They can also destroy a firm if they suck up more resources than it can afford.

Pro bono tips:

- Stay in charge of the volume of your pro bono work by controlling when you work for free or at a reduced rate
- Establish the number of pro bono files you are willing to take on, and stick to it
- Keep a written list of your pro bono files and refer to it before opening a new one so you don't get too many
- Get the backing of someone with authority before starting a new pro bono file (the firm has a stake in your pro bono work)
- Carefully evaluate the work a new pro bono file requires
- Manage your pro bono client's expectations very carefully because their instructions will not be tempered by the need to pay for the work they ask you to do
- Assess the character of your pro bono clients carefully so a decision to take on a difficult client is made consciously
- Record time spent on your pro bono files

Private practice financial tips

This section is for those of you going into private practice.

- Every time you get a new client, discuss the basis on which your fees are calculated at the first interview. If the client decides that the proposed services are too expensive, be glad you found out at the beginning of the file rather than at the end when the work has been done, the client is refusing to pay and you have to explain to the firm why the account has gone bad

• Put your fee arrangements in writing
• If you are assigned a file on which there is a question of the client's willingness or ability to pay, discuss the issue of payment with the assigning lawyer so you are both clear about how much the firm expects to be paid and how you will get credit for your work
• Whenever possible and appropriate, get a retainer
• Keep meticulous time records, whether you bill by the hour or not
• Don't let your unbilled disbursements get out of control
• Use an aged work-in-progress report to keep your billings current
• Interim bill whenever feasible
• Use an aged accounts receivable report to keep on top of the money that is owing on your work; if a client misses a payment, follow up personally and quickly; if the client is no longer willing or able to pay, cease working on the file unless you decide consciously to continue working for nothing

> Law schools don't teach anything about the business of law, so most private firms don't expect entrepreneurial skills in their new lawyers. You can make an excellent impression by establishing effective financial management in your own practice right away.

Well, what should I do?

You may be tempted to shy away from the financial side of practice in your early years in the profession and instead just put your head down and practice law. You may be encouraged in this attitude by higher-ups who do not think you should concern yourself with such matters. However, you will be judged, at least in part, on the basis of your financial contribution to the organization in which you work, so you should keep track of the basic information you will need to prove that you are a good investment.

In a private practice law firm, your production will be judged by your billings and/or collections. In a quick-turnaround transactional practice, billings and collections are as good a gauge as any. You should therefore keep track of how much is billed and collected as a result of your work, including fees you bill yourself and those hidden in the billings of others. If you work on longer-term files that are not billed regularly (for example, contingency files), you should monitor your billable hours as well as your billings so you get appropriate credit for all your work.

To keep track of your production:

- Start a ledger book or computer file (a spreadsheet or table) in which you record all fees billed for your work, including fees billed by you and those hidden in the billings of others
- Check entries off when the money comes in
- Each month, summarize your billable time, non-billable time, fees billed, fees collected, unbilled work-in-progress and accounts receivable
- Chart your monthly information to see trends and patterns

In other types of legal organizations, production measures are likely to be less clear-cut, and one of your tasks as a new lawyer is to find out how you are to be evaluated. Once you know what is important to the organization, you can keep track of everything that shows evidence of your contribution.

Chapter 7

Time Management

The goal of time management is to increase your productivity, to increase the amount of work you get done in a given amount of time. The best strategies for achieving that goal are focus and organization.

Four steps to improving your time management

Four actions, repeatedly endorsed throughout the time management literature, can help you focus and organize:

1. Use a written (or computerized) To-Do list
You will overload your memory if you try to keep everything you have to do in your head. It's also a bad idea to use files, letters or yellow stickies to remind you of things you need to do. Instead, make a list of all your pending jobs.

> **6 6**There is no such thing as time management, there is only self-management. Everyone has all the time there is; people who get more done manage themselves better. It's all a matter of personal discipline.**9 9**
> —PAUL MCLAUGHLIN

> **6 6**If you had to identify, in one word, the reason why the human race has not achieved, and never will achieve, its full potential, that word would be: "meetings".**9 9**
> —DAVE BARRY,
> *Dave Barry Turns 50*

> In the past, To-Do lists were kept on paper, which meant they had to be recreated every day. Now you can use a computer, which is much more efficient. Changing a date or priority is a simple drag-and-drop operation. The time you take to learn the features of your personal information management software will be amply rewarded.

2. Prioritize
It's not enough to just have a list; the list needs to be **structured** so you can determine what to do first, what to do next, and what not to do at all. Start with the most important item and work on it until it is done. Do not let yourself be distracted. If a crisis occurs, assess whether solving the crisis is

truly more important than completing the item you are working on. When you complete an item, pause and decide whether you need to revise your list. If something has come up that is more important than the next item on your list, write it at the top of the list and do it. Otherwise, write it in the appropriate place on your list and proceed with the next highest priority item.

A To-Do list should be do-able in one day. Don't work from a list of 25 or 30 items because you will not get them all done. Time does not miraculously appear during the day. Review your list first thing in the morning, pare it down to a reasonable size, and commit yourself to finishing everything you leave on it.

See page 72 for a Daily Plan form you can use to prioritize your day.

3. Customize
The particulars of how you list and prioritize your work do not matter, as long as your system works for you.

4. Form effective habits
Time management should become as habitual as driving. When you are about to turn, you don't think about putting on your directional signal, you just do it. Similarly, when you decide something needs to be done, you shouldn't have to think about writing it down, you should just do it.

66Habit is the flywheel of society, its most precious conserving agent. . . . We must make automatic and habitual, as early as possible, as many useful actions as we can. . . . The more of the details of our daily life we can hand over to the effortless custody of automatism, the more our higher powers of mind will be set free for their proper work. There is no more miserable person than one in whom nothing is habitual.**99**

—William James

Set priorities according to the importance of the task, not the pleasure you will receive from doing it. If anything, assign unpleasant tasks a higher priority than pleasant ones.

When scheduling your day, don't forget to leave time for the phone calls and other interruptions that will inevitably occur throughout the day.

Forming excellent time management habits takes four steps:

1. Acquire **knowledge** about time management theory and practice by reading, observing and listening
2. Evolve a positive **attitude** toward time management and a hearty dislike for disorganization, crisis and procrastination
3. Develop your time management **skills,** such as prioritizing, concentrating and following through
4. Persist until good time management **habits** are second nature to you

> Reversing bad time management habits can be as hard for the terminally disorganised lawyer as quitting smoking is for the commited, pack-a-day smoker.

It takes a long time to entrench good time management habits, years if poor time management habits are deeply ingrained. But persevere, because it is worth it.

Scheduling uninterrupted time

To cut down on interruptions, schedule uninterrupted time for specific projects that require extra concentration. For example, if you have to draft a claim, book three hours next Tuesday morning starting at 8:00 a.m. Put it in your appointments calendar. Put your phone on "Do Not Disturb". Advise the receptionist that you intend to return calls between 11:00 and 12:00. Change your voice-mail message so people know you intend to call them back before noon. Set an alarm on your computer and take your watch off. Find a quiet place to work or close your door. Then go to work and work hard until the time is up.

Projects that can't be completed in one sitting are dangerous if you keep putting them off. Recognize that you'll never have a day when you have enough time to do the whole thing at once and schedule several specific blocks of time instead.

You may be concerned that clients will be offended by this approach. However, most clients can live with the fact that there are times when they can't get in touch with you, such as when you are in court or with a client. Just because you are in the office, it doesn't follow that they have a right to unconditional access, as long **as you get back to them as soon as your uninterrupted block is over**.

> The time management literature consists of **systems** and **tips**. Adopt tips that fit your personality and work habits, even if you don't like the author's system.

You also risk offending colleagues who want to chat. Advise them that you have committed yourself to getting this work done this morning but will be glad to talk about last night's game over lunch. They will soon realize that when you close your office door, you really don't want to be disturbed and will leave you alone.

Time management tips

1. Take a time management course whenever you get a chance. You'll always learn something new and you'll experience a renewed enthusiasm for improving your time management habits when you spend time with others who are committed to improving theirs

2. If you are in charge of a meeting:
   - Prepare and distribute the agenda and agenda material beforehand

- Start on time (to the minute—do not reward tardiness)
- Announce the finish time at the beginning
- Stick to the agenda
- Do not give people permission to take up meeting time to read the agenda material
- End on time
- Prepare and distribute minutes immediately

> If you don't have time for your family and for yourself, you're not managing your time well.

3. Observe what you can get done when you have a deadline. For example, make a mental note of how much work you can crank out in the last two or three days before you leave on vacation, then use that as a benchmark every day. (Do not apply this tip if the way you get a lot done just before a vacation is by working excessive hours.)

4. Use voice mail and e-mail

5. Leave yourself voice-mail messages when you are out of the office

6. Identify your productive and non-productive times of the day and try to schedule your most difficult tasks during your most productive times

7. Complete at least one non-urgent task every day

8. How to handle incoming mail:
   - Set a specific time each day to go through the mail (if you can't wait, discipline yourself to deal with it as quickly as possible and don't let yourself be more than momentarily sidetracked from your priority list)
   - Don't have the file pulled until you decide whether you need it (see Chapter 1, "How to Make Friends with Your Files")

• Go through the mail methodically; if you can't deal with an item within **one minute** by dictating a quick instruction or response, put it on your To-Do list

> Some of your most valuable time is spent on activities that don't appear to make you busy—thinking, creating, analyzing and planning. Make sure you schedule time for these important activities.

9. If a crisis knocks your time management off kilter, do what you have to, then get back on track as soon as possible. If you have crises every day, you are not managing your time well.

A difficult problem

How do you deal with the undisciplined senior lawyer who considers it a prerogative of tenure, not to mention a good growth experience for you, to hammer you with emergencies that must be dealt with immediately, ignoring the fact that you have other deadlines? Let's say one of these inconsiderate boors drops a bomb on your desk on Wednesday and tells you it has to be defused by Thursday at the latest, although it has been ticking away on a credenza for two months. You could say, "I would be glad to do the work, but I already have three Thursday deadlines and so I won't be able to get everything done on time. Would you please explain to the other lawyers I have to work for, why their work won't get done on time." To carry this off, you must have **detailed** information about your current workload **at your fingertips**. Although it may cause some unpleasantness, standing up to such lack of consideration will be a better growth experience for you in the long run than knuckling under.

Well, what should I do?

First, be alert to the dangers of **time heroism**. You will come across lawyers who brag about working incredibly long hours. They are not heroic, they are foolish. Your ability to function at a high level declines dramatically after eight hours. If you know you are going to work into the evening, you'll be less disciplined during the day because you know that you can always finish your work later. You'll also be less energetic during the day because you will be storing up resources for your after-hours stint. In some legal organizations, there is enormous pressure to engage in this foolishness. You'll be better off if you resist the pressure and instead try to organize your work so you finish it during normal business hours.

> If you work long hours, your boss may conclude that you don't know how to organize your work well.

Second, watch for signs of **adrenaline addiction**. If you leave things to the last minute, revel in crisis, and ignore tasks that don't generate an immediate rush, you may have established a pattern in which procrastination is a necessary ingredient in your enjoyment of life. You may complain about stress and frustration, but you actually reward yourself psychologically by making yourself the center of attention. You cast yourself as the hero because everyone depends on you to pull the situation out of the fire, but you are responsible for the fire in the first place.

On the positive side, a collateral benefit of good time management is a reputation for reliability, which makes your life as a lawyer infinitely easier. Clients who know they can count on you are happy to refer their friends and colleagues, and other lawyers like working with you because your dealings are based on trust, not suspicion.

> ❝Years ago when I first started out as a consultant, I had to learn how to tell a well-managed industrial plant from a poorly managed one—without any pretence to production knowledge. A well-managed plant, I soon learned, is a quiet place. A factory that is "dramatic", a factory in which the "epic of the century" is unfolded before the visitor's eyes, is poorly managed. A well-managed factory is boring. Nothing exciting happens in it because the crises have been anticipated and have been converted into routine.❞
>
> —Peter Drucker,
> *The Effective Executive*

Daily Plan

Date:

Must Do Priorities: **Must Call Priorities:**

☐ _____   ☐

☐ _____   ☐

☐ _____   ☐

☐ _____   ☐

☐ _____   ☐

Files to be dealt with:

    Name of File: To Do:

☐ _____

☐ _____

☐ _____

☐ _____

☐ _____

☐ _____

Scheduled Events:

    Matter: Time/Notes:

☐ _____

☐ _____

☐ _____

☐ _____

☐ _____

Chapter 8

Keeping Your Toes Out of Ethical Hot Water

You now have the opportunity—and responsibility—to apply your ethical education.

Law schools have made a concerted effort in the past decade to increase the amount of time spent on professionalism, but it is hard to teach ethics in the academy because hypothetical ethical dilemmas just aren't real enough to be prepare you for what you now face. Problems that seemed easy to resolve in the classroom turn out to be much more difficult, and interesting, out here in the real world.

Ethical rules are not designed to trap you or limit your freedom of action; they are common-sense tools intended to help you figure out how to deal professionally with everyone you come into contact with in your professional capacity—your clients, other lawyers, the courts and anyone else.

You will be well on your way to keeping your toes out of ethical hot water if you remember the following five "C-words": Confidentiality, Commitment, Candor, Civility and Competence.

Confidentiality

Confidentiality is the bedrock of the lawyer-client relationship. It is impossible to overstate the importance of

> 66 Lawyers who know how to think but have not learned how to behave are a menace and a liability not an asset to the administration of justice. 99
>
> —Warren E. Burger

> 66 Being a practicing professional means being ready to be held accountable for your actions. 99
>
> —Paul McLaughlin

To maintain confidentiality:
- Don't gossip about your cases or your clients
- Don't talk about your cases within earshot of people who should not be privy to the information (including people in your legal organization who don't need to know about the case to do their jobs)
- Don't leave your files lying around the house, in your car or in public places where someone inappropriate may see them
- Don't write confidential information (addresses, phone numbers) on the outside of your file folders

the rule that you must keep secret all information you receive about your clients' business, interests and affairs.

For all practical purposes, you should consider everything you learn about your clients in the course of your professional relationship to be *prima facie* confidential.

The confidentiality obligation is not absolute. Reasons that may justify disclosure include a legal obligation, prevention of a future crime and an express or implied waiver from your client. When disclosure is justified, you must disclose as little information as possible.

The ethical rule of confidentiality vs. the law of privilege

The **ethical rule of confidentiality** governs your conduct as a lawyer when you possess information obtained in the course of representing a client, including privileged information. In certain circumstances, a tribunal can order you to disclose confidential, non-privileged information. Confidentiality is enforced and protected through the disciplinary processes of the law society or state bar association.

The **law of privilege** governs the compellability of certain types of evidence in proceedings before tribunals. You cannot be ordered to give up privileged information. The range of information protected by privilege is narrower than that covered by confidentiality, and the exceptions are different. Privilege is enforced and protected by the courts and other tribunals in the course of litigation.

* * *

If a judge presses you to disclose information you consider to be confidential or privileged, say, "Your Honor, I must respectfully decline to disclose that information because it would contravene my duty of confidentiality / privilege to my client."

If the judge persists, ask for an adjournment to seek legal and ethical advice.

If your client consents to the disclosure, the consent must be fully informed and voluntary and your disclosure must not mislead.

Commitment

The rule that you must be committed to your clients' interests encompasses the conflict of interest rules and the duty of zealous representation.

The conflict of interest rules are rooted in the idea that you must give your undivided loyalty to your clients. You can't act on both sides of a dispute. You can't use clients' confidential information against them. You can't put your personal loyalties, family ties, financial interests, personal beliefs or outside activities ahead of your clients' interests. Your clients come first; if you can't live with that in a particular case, you must cease acting for that client.

As the profession has struggled to deal with multiple representation, mobility and law firm mergers, changing times have made the conflict of interest rules more complex than they were in the past. Nevertheless, the underlying principles have remained the same and the courts have taken a firm stand against any weakening of the protections clients enjoy under the conflict rules.

The rule of zealous representation requires you to do your utmost to advance your clients' interests in your advocacy. It is a positive duty. It is qualified, however, by your legal and ethical obligations, including the duty of civility. A client cannot instruct you to act illegally or unethically. Although consideration of this duty most often arises in the context of litigation, it applies to any situation in which you are acting as an advocate.

Candor

The essence of this principle can be summed up in two words: Don't lie.

Don't lie to your clients. Don't lie to other lawyers. Don't lie to the courts. Don't lie to the public. Don't lie by commission. Don't lie by omission. Don't lie, period.

The duty of candor also requires you to keep your clients informed about what is going on in their files. You cannot keep bad news from clients, even when you know they will be distressed. Letting your clients know if you have made a mistake is one of the most difficult things you have to do as a lawyer.

Here are some tips on delivering bad news:
- Don't put it off
- Arrange to meet with the client in person; don't send a letter or make a phone call
- If the client is likely to become belligerent, have another person in the room with you
- Be candid and objective
- Don't try to excuse the problem away
- Acknowledge the impact of the bad news and be prepared for the client to react emotionally
- Let the client know he or she can get another lawyer to review the file
- Let the client know he or she can take the file to another firm if there has been a loss of confidence
- Don't charge for the meeting if you are reporting a mistake you have made

Civility

Lawyers often get involved in extreme situations. When the stakes are high, tempers can flare and stress levels can soar. The duty of civility requires you to remain courteous, even when everyone else in the room is losing it.

Once again, the rules are simple. Don't be rude or insult people or call them names. Don't needle people. Don't boss people around. Say "Please" and "Thank you." Don't yell as a weapon of intimidation. Speak respectfully.

The duty of civility extends beyond the courtroom; it applies to all your dealings with clients, the courts, other lawyers and members of the public.

The duty of civility is sometimes thought to be in conflict with the duty of zealous representation. In fact, it's not. Some of the most effective advocates are also the calmest, most courteous people you would like to meet. They are effective because they focus on their clients' long-term strategic goals and don't sabotage themselves or their clients with destructive short-term tactics.

One consequence of the duty of civility is that you must accommodate opposing counsel when they request waivers of procedural formality, although you must not sacrifice your clients' legal interests to meet such requests. For example, if you are in a position to enter default judgment and your client has instructed you not to make any concessions to the other side, you are still obliged to grant a reasonable extension of the time for filing a defense if an application to set the default judgment aside would inevitably succeed. You are not required to extend time, however, if the effect of doing so would be to waive a limitation period that your client is entitled to rely on.

Competence

The duty of competence requires you to be capable of doing the legal work you take on, and to decline work that is beyond your abilities or refer it to someone else. You don't have to be competent in everything that a lawyer might be called on to do, but you are required to be on top of the areas of law in which you practice. You are also expected to know and respect your limits.

You can accept a file that is presently beyond your abilities if, without undue cost to the client, you can bring yourself up to speed within a reasonable time or bring in more expert counsel.

The law is constantly changing, so a corollary of the duty of competence is ongoing self-education, either on your own or through continuing legal education programs. If you're licensed in a jurisdiction with mandatory continuing legal education, you have to comply with the local MCLE rules.

Another corollary is that you should seek help if your capacity or motivation is impaired by excessive use of alcohol or drugs, overwork, personal problems, health problems or involvement in outside activities. If the impairment is severe, you may have to withdraw from practice. All law societies in Canada and state bars in the United States have programs to help lawyers with these kinds of difficulties. They are typically free, at least for the initial consultation, and confidential.

Providing competent legal services involves more than just getting the right answers to legal questions. It also requires you to be conscientious, diligent and efficient in the delivery of those services. In other words, you have to manage your practice so you get your work done in a timely fashion.

The Barry Vogel take on legal ethics

Barry Vogel is the Practice Advisor at the Law Society of Alberta. He was a member of a Committee that undertook a massive, seven-year revision of Alberta's Code of Professional Conduct. At the end of it all, Barry produced a verse rendition of the Code. He had this to say about the relationship of the lawyer to society and the justice system:

> We act with much propriety
> With dignity and piety
> Shunning notoriety
> As we serve society.
>
> In this Code we list 'em
> So you can't say you missed 'em
> Rules expounding wisdom
> To serve the Justice System.

He reduced many years of discussion and debate on confidentiality to this:

> News will always spread eventually
> When you start with, "Confidentially".
> There is nothing more absurd
> Than saying, "Don't repeat a word".

Resist temptation to regale
Your colleagues with that juicy tale.
The best way to protect your butt
Is always keep your big mouth shut!

After the Committee agonized over what to say about the
lawyer as advisor, Barry chimed in with:

When you're advising clients
You'll want to be objective.
Remember that their memories
Are often quite selective.

They'll say that what you said was "black"
And that's what starts the fighting.
To prove that what you said was "white"
Make sure that it's in writing.

The liberal Alberta rules on advertising didn't escape the
Vogel wit:

Patronize our law firm.
Service with a smile.
And for every dollar spent
A frequent flyer mile.

Here's our current special
(Just this week, of course):
Let us do your injury claim.
We'll throw in a divorce.

Why don't you come along!
The throng of clients marches
Into our reception room
Beneath the Golden Arches.

We'll serve you tea or coffee
And feed your little bellies.
And while we're on the subject,
Have you tried our jams and jellies?

In all our advertising
There only is one flaw.
We don't know how to tell you
We're here to practice law!

Finally, what do you say about the client you who doesn't pay
your bill?

Your client has just fired you
And hasn't paid your bill.
He never did cooperate
And likely never will.

A month from now he'll plead with you
To help him through the mess.
You know that you'll get beat again.
But still you will say, "Yes".

Who says ethics can't be poetic?

Well, what should I do?

If there is one piece of practical ethical advice that stands out from the rest, it is this:

Don't try to resolve ethical problems in isolation.

Although lawyers are in economic competition with each other, practicing law is still a collegial activity, particularly when it comes to talking through ethical problems. Seek out ethical mentors in your organization or your local bar. If your law society or state bar has an ethics hotline or an opinion service, use it. Talk to your friends and classmates. Talk to an intelligent non-lawyer; sometimes the insights of someone who is not a member of the profession can provide a good perspective.

When you're satisfied that you have a full understanding of the principles involved, make your decision and implement it. If you think your decision may be challenged, make a record of your discussions and the reasons for your decision.

Chapter 9

Write Right

Good writing skills will stand you in good stead throughout your legal career. They will also help you in anything else you choose to do in life.

> ❝Language is both a tool and a weapon. Those who can use this gift effectively have a powerful advantage.❞
>
> — ALBERT JOSEPH,
> *Executive Guide to Grammar*

When you complete a written assignment as a lawyer, you lose control over who sees it. It may be seen by clients, other lawyers and their clients, and other people with an interest in them. Everything you write has the potential to end up in the public domain, and thus be open to perusal by members of the general public, including journalists.

Legal documents often take on lives of their own. They are studied and relied upon by contractual parties; fought over by will trustees and beneficiaries; submitted to, argued about and interpreted by judges; searched and copied in public registries; and saved as precedents to be used in the future by new lawyers who are in the same situation you are in. Your documents may even be quoted in judgments and become part of common law.

> ❝Thinking is the process of simplifying the relationships between ideas. Therefore, simplicity is not only desirable—it is the mark of the thinking person.❞
>
> —ALBERT JOSEPH,
> *Executive Guide to Grammar*

Many legal documents reach a critical point in time when they become irrevocable, usually by being executed or by being filed or registered in a public office. The few documents that can be pulled back when an error is discovered can usually be revised only at the cost of considerable embarrassment. So they have to be right. You should never, never, never produce any written work that is less than excellent.

> Before you finalize anything you write, ask yourself if you would be willing to have it attached to an affidavit and filed in court.

Excellent writing starts long before you actually start putting the words together. The preliminaries include a thorough understanding of the purpose of the document and the context in which it will be used, good research and investigation and sound analysis.

When you get an assignment

Your commitment to writing excellence starts when you first get a new assignment. Remember to:

- Get as many facts as you can before you leave the assigning lawyer's office
- Ask about the context of the assignment—What is the file about? Who are the parties? Who do you represent? What stage has the file reached? What role does your work play in resolving it?
- Get suggestions about where to start
- Ask whether the assigning lawyer is aware of any precedent materials in the library, computer system or other files
- If you don't already know, find out how the assigning lawyer wants the assignment formatted; ask for samples of similar assignments that the assigning lawyer thinks were well done and use them as models
- Find out if there is a time or billing budget for the assignment
- Find out the assigning lawyer's expectations about how deep you are to dig
- Establish a mutually acceptable deadline, bearing in mind that assignments normally take three to five times longer than assigning lawyers and eager associates initially anticipate

- Immediately enter the assignment in your To-Do list and, if appropriate, schedule a block of time to work on it
- Immediately do something to get the assignment launched

As you work on the assignment

Your commitment to excellence continues as you work on the project. Here are some tips to help you along the way:

- Before you start your research, develop a written plan or checklist that identifies, in a preliminary way, the issues involved in the assignment and the facts and law needed to complete it
- As early as possible in the process, ask as many questions as you need to
- Compile a list of questions and get them all answered at the same time rather than going back to the assigning lawyer with each concern
- Try to anticipate the questions your research will raise in the mind of the assigning lawyer
- Keep an eye on the big picture and don't get bogged down in the minutiae
- In your planning, leave some time for the assignment to bounce around in your subconscious; you'll often find that time spent working on something else results in unexpected insights
- Talk about the assignment with fellow associates, classmates and anyone else who might be interested, being careful not to disclose any confidential information (be careful because sometimes disclosure of the fact that you are working on the assignment can be damaging to the client)

- Set interim deadlines and revise your plan or checklist as you proceed
- Let the assigning lawyer know as soon as possible if his or her expectations about the deadline, the complexity of the assignment or the budget are turning out to be unrealistic
- Treat the assignment as an opportunity to learn new facts and law and to develop your skills as a lawyer
- Apply your critical judgment to the assignment and come out with an answer or recommendation, not just a recital of the facts and the law
- Go beyond what is asked of you
- Leave enough time to get the word processing done without undue pressure on others

When writing

Now you get down to the actual writing.

Some tips to keep in mind:

- Plan your document; create an outline but don't be a slave to it
- Schedule an appointment for yourself to write your first draft (you can edit a document in installments, but you need a block of uninterrupted time to get your first draft down on paper)
- Be focused; don't ramble on about tangentially related points
  - Use plain language

There is no good writing; there is only good rewriting.

  - Use titles, subtitles and paragraph numbers to structure your document
  - Use a table of contents

- When you quote from court decisions, quote only the words you need to make your point; leave out all the nice-sounding but superfluous judicial verbiage and supply context concisely in your own words

  > When a client asks for a cheese sandwich, don't explain how to raise cows.

- Shape your language according to the purpose of the assignment; for example, in an opinion on the likelihood of the success of a motion or an action, you can use qualified language, but in a brief to be filed in court, state your points affirmatively and unconditionally

  > Legal opinions are not short stories; you don't have to build suspense.

- If your document is an opinion, come to the point quickly—state the problem and put your conclusion in the first paragraph, not the last

When finalizing the assignment

Your document is about to go out of your control and become irrevocable. Is it ready? Will it make you proud or embarrass you? In the last stages of revision, remember to:

- Re-read the document to make sure that it is grammatically correct, that the language flows smoothly and that the argument, if there is one, is carefully structured and can be easily followed
- Ask yourself if your document makes sense
- Proofread and spell-check (you should do this with every piece of paper that goes out with your name on it)
- Check all your citations
- Make sure the document looks good

Wordsmithery
by Paul McLaughlin

Here are some helpful tips to use when you hammer your writing into shape on the old verbal anvil.

- First, foremost and above all, be very, very, very, extra careful to avoid repetitious, superfluous, auxiliary, redundant words that say the same thing two or three times. And sentence fragments that begin with contractions.

- It's kind of important to be sort of clear and rather precise in choosing subjects for your sentences.

- You ought not to thoughtlessly generalize, because only one writer in a billion can use exaggeration effectively, but it's never a good idea to carelessly split an infinitive, especially in a run-on sentence that never seems to ever end, and a preposition is a poor word to end a sentence with.

- Next rule, make sure your verb agree with their subjects.

- The passive voice is to be avoided like the plague, as are old, tired, worn-out, old-hat cliches, even if you put "quotation marks" around them. And remember, even if a mixed metaphor gets off the launching pad, it won't necessarily make it to the White House.

- Don't use contractions, abbreviations & ampersands, etc.

- Its important to study the apostrophe and it's proper use. And don't use one word sentences. Ever.

- Use commas, carefully, and avoid them where, they are not required. However parenthetical words though like, however, should (nevertheless) always be enclosed in commas [moreover].

- Never use no double negatives, or foreign words that are prima facie. And what good are rhetorical questions? Or big words and high-sounding phrases when minuscule ones are sufficient unto the day?

- Don't inventify old concepts into new words.

- Remember: a pun in a formal document is like a shoe tree in a running shoe—the last thing you'd expect. And a pun in a written complaint is like a sausage in a seafood salad—the wurst thing to find when you are looking for a crab.

- A metaphor is a simile you don't "like".

- Colloquialisms just, like, you know, stink, and to hell with crude language.

- Avoid sarcasm; you probably wouldn't recognize it anyway.

- Eliminate excessive exclamation marks: they just clutter up the page. And absolutely abandon all attempts at affectatious alliteration!!!

- Finally, prove reed all your work cheerfully because spell checkers sometimes muss thongs.

Following completion of the assignment

It's not over yet. Even after you have completed your assignment, there is still much you can learn if you seek feedback. It may be painful, and you have to be persistent, but you will improve more quickly if you always insist on comments from the assigning lawyer.

> In assessing feedback, distinguish between substantive points and esthetic preferences.

Finally, follow up to see what impact your work had on the case. Knowing the impact of your work is an essential ingredient in developing judgment.

Well, what should I do?

Writing is a skill, so no matter how good you are, you can improve through practice. There are many ways to do so:

- Take a plain writing course and implement what you learn
- When you come across a legal document that you feel is particularly well-written, study it to see if you can identify what the author has done to make it stand out
- Don't be a slave to precedent
- Read your drafts out loud to see what they will "sound like" in the minds of readers
- Adapt your writing style to your audience
- Practice, practice, practice

Chapter 10

How to Make Yourself Indispensable

The premise of this chapter is that you have decided to make your career, or at least the next foreseeable part of it, in the organization in which you are presently working. If you are at odds with your organization, you probably won't like the advice in this chapter and you should read Chapter 11, "Planning Your Career", right away.

Find out what your organization values and deliver it

If you want a positive long-term relationship with your organization, you have to deliver what it values.

From this it follows that one of your primary tasks as a new lawyer is to discern what really matters in your organization. Some organizations are clear about their focus, but others are not. At best, they put out conflicting messages; at worst, they are inwardly focused and unprincipled. For example, you may have been told during your interview that the organization has a strong commitment to client service, but once you become part of the organization, you discover that in fact the lawyers who are committed to client service have little real influence and that, overall, client service comes a distant second behind billing as many hours as possible.

It may take some time, but when you have it sorted out, you can start to shape your practice so it contributes effectively to

> ❝The effective executive focuses on contribution. . . . The great majority of executives tend to focus downward. They are occupied with efforts rather than with results. They worry over what the organization and their superiors 'owe' them and should do for them. And they are conscious above all of the authority they 'should have.' As a result, they render themselves ineffectual. . . . The focus on contribution turns the executive's attention away from his [or her] own specialty, his [or her] own narrow skills, his [or her] own department, and toward the performance of the whole. . . . Executives who do not ask themselves, 'What can I contribute?' are not only likely to aim too low, they are likely to aim at the wrong things. Above all, they may define their contribution too narrowly.❞
>
> —Peter F. Drucker,
> *The Effective Executive*

the achievement of the organization's goals—or you can decide that the organization doesn't deliver what you need and move on.

> To get a sense of what your organization expects from you, check out the performance evaluation process. Who will be doing your evaluation? What is the timing and format? Is there a form? What is the evaluation used for? Is it taken seriously or is it just a formality?

Most legal organizations support new lawyers who want to make contributions other than the production of legal work, such as scholarly writing, pro bono cases, participation in professional organizations, public or professional education, in firm social activities, marketing, etc. Make sure the support is genuine: some firms pay lip service to collateral contributions, but at evaluation time, they turn out to only be interested in financial contributions.

> Peter Drucker invented the science of management. In *The Effective Executive* (Harper & Rowe, 1966), he says that to be effective, knowledge workers like lawyers should focus on making a contribution by helping their organizations make a valued difference to their clients. In other words, they should direct their efforts toward achieving results for the organization rather than just doing the work that is assigned to them.

Don't join the counter-culture

Every organization larger than about ten people develops a counter-culture—a group of people who don't accept the prevailing conventional wisdom. They are the complainers and trouble-makers, the chronic skeptics who roll their eyes when management tries to make an appeal to positive values. New employees sometimes find these cynics attractive because they seem so knowledgeable and witty. However, if you want to get ahead in an organization, you are well advised to steer clear of them. The leadership knows who they are and will not be impressed if you decide to associate with them.

Promote the interests of the organization

Here are some ways to promote the interests of your organization:

• Work hard
• Don't bad-mouth the organization, internally or externally
• If you have a complaint, handle it discreetly, not publicly
• Promote new business for other lawyers in the organization
• Brag about the good things the organization does
• Participate in the organization's charitable and promotional activities

Constantly improve your knowledge

Although you have graduated from law school, your legal education is only just beginning. From now on, however, it is your responsibility. There are plenty of ways to expand your knowledge, develop your skills and keep abreast of new developments:

Read. Read case law, legal newspapers, legal magazines, legal textbooks, histories of the law and the legal profession, and biographies and autobiographies of lawyers. By reading widely, you subtly deepen your understanding of the interconnectedness of the law and become increasingly confident in your judgment about whether a legal proposition makes sense.

Go to seminars. Every jurisdiction on the continent offers extensive continuing legal education programming. If you practice in a jurisdiction with mandatory continuing legal edu-

> Don't be afraid to take a seminar outside your area of concentration.

cation, you won't have a choice, but even if continuing legal education is not compulsory, attend as many educational programs as you can.

Observe. There is so much to be learned from watching the masters at work. The early years of your practice are your best opportunity to take the time to sit in court and watch a superb cross-examination or jury address, to sit in a meeting and watch a skillful negotiator, to sit in the law library and try to follow the mental processes of an excellent researcher. When you get busier, you won't have these opportunities.

Write. One of the best ways to extend your understanding of an area of practice is to write articles on legal topics.

Teach. Teaching is a great way to improve your understanding of the law. You may not be ready to teach law students or lawyers, but there is no reason why you can't teach at a community college, trade school or high school during the day or in evening classes. You can also give seminars to non-lawyers.

> An academic article articulates the subtleties of a subject for lawyers. An article for a lay audience must express the essence of the law clearly—an excellent discipline and a good learning experience.

For example, you can do an important public service by teaching board members of nonprofit organizations about the duties of officers, directors and employees; the importance of liability insurance; and basic corporate, tax, trust, employment, insurance, charity and general liability law. You'll have to brush up on these topics yourself, adding detail to the outline understanding you acquired in law school. You also get collateral benefits in the form of excellent public exposure for you and your firm.

Make every assignment a learning experience. Every new assignment involves new facts, new people and the potential for new legal subtleties. Even if an assignment does not challenge you with new knowledge, it can help you increase your skill.

Learn from your mistakes. No one expects you to be perfect, so you don't need to expect it of yourself. However, you must learn from your mistakes and not make them again. When you make a mistake, tell someone right away. You will feel better and you may stop the situation from getting worse.

Market yourself internally

The essence of marketing is this: search the marketplace for needs that you want to fill, then position yourself to form relationships with the people who have the needs so they want to give you work. When you are a new lawyer, one of the main sources of your work is likely to be other lawyers in the same organization. Since they are your market, you need to ask yourself about their needs. At one level, they are the same as the needs of all potential clients: timeliness, quality, reliability, personal attention, sound judgment, trust and integrity. At another level, however, their needs are unique. It is up to you, as a seller of your services, to figure out the particular needs of the lawyers who can provide you with work, and then to position yourself to be the obvious choice to meet their needs.

For example, if would like to work with a tax lawyer who, to your knowledge, has a problem with procrastination, you could show up every Friday afternoon and ask for a dog file that you could get back on the rails. It doesn't matter if you are interested in the contents of the file because the point is not to get good work, it is to show the tax lawyer that you have good skills and work habits and that you are interested in tax work. In other words, you want to establish a relationship. It may take some time, and you may have to plow through an awful pile of tedious files before you start getting the good stuff, but if you show yourself to be useful and trustworthy, you will begin to receive more interesting assignments (unless, of course, you chose your target poorly).

Take control of your practice

One of the most powerful ways to impress your superiors is to take immediate, absolute control of your practice.

Encourage your assistant to develop good relationships with other lawyers and their assistants; court clerks and other government employees; and service providers such as couriers, process servers, and court reporters.

As you get busier, it gets increasingly difficult to keep your practice under control. You have two choices: work harder or work smarter. Working smarter is always better. You should think of yourself as a manager who is responsible for getting your work done, not a production worker who is responsible for doing the work. Working smarter requires you to:

- **Organize** everything: your work, your time, your space, your tools, your files—everything
- **Delegate** everything you can to the appropriate level of expertise
- **Use technology** wherever you can

See Chapter 3, "Let's Get Personal about Practice Management", for information on how to make personal practice management decisions. Here are a dozen more personal practice management tips:

1. Keep a file list so you always know all the files you are working on
2. Keep a list of important clients' phone numbers and addresses on your desk or in your computer
3. Use a prioritized To-Do list religiously
4. Use checklists whenever possible
5. Don't set deadlines you won't be able to meet, and revise deadlines as necessary so they remain realistic
6. Learn how to use your organization's conflict of interest, limitations and calendar systems
7. Proof-read every piece of paper that goes out of your office
8. Return all phone calls promptly
9. Don't let files pile up in your office and don't let your filing get behind
10. Learn how to use your organization's file tickler system
11. Don't keep clients waiting for appointments
12. Bill promptly and follow up assertively on accounts receivable

Learn to say "No"

This is one of the most important lessons a new lawyer can learn, but also one of the hardest. Far too many lawyers at all levels of seniority are overwhelmed with work and other commitments because they lack the capacity to utter a simple, one-syllable, two-letter word. If you cave in every time someone asks you to do something, your lack of spine will begin to raise questions about what you do when clients, other lawyers and judges lean on you, as they inevitably will.

You learn a lot about yourself and about the organization in which you work when you draw a reasoned line in the sand. Legal organizations should appreciate new lawyers who stand up for themselves, but many don't. For example, you may refuse to alter your plans when asked to work through a weekend because of an emergency created entirely by a senior lawyer's procrastination. Taking this stand may produce a crisis in your relationship with the organization. You may have to move on, but both you and the organization will then be better off, because you will have a chance to find a place to work that is more consistent with your values, and the organization will be able to replace you with someone who is a better fit for its profile.

You may be able to change a "No" into a "Yes, but not now. How about next week when I have finished the work I am already committed to?"

Of course, you can't just say "No" arbitrarily. You have to learn when to say it, how to say it and how to articulate your reasons and defend your decisions. See page 70 in Chapter 7, "Time Management."

If your efforts to assert yourself are repeatedly squashed, you are not getting the essential support you need to develop into a self-confident lawyer and it may be time to move on. See Chapter 11, "Planning Your Career."

Be nice to the people you work with

Re-read Chapter 4 on working with your assistant and extend the same civility to others in your organization. Remember to:

- Say "Good Morning" and "Good Night"
- Say "Please" and "Thank you"
- Acknowledge birthdays, graduations and other milestones
- Give credit to others for their contributions to your success
- Be particularly nice to the receptionist
- Make a fuss when someone performs above and beyond expectations
- Don't lie and don't expect others to lie for you
- Realize that sometimes a leader must be a follower
- Be a realist, but don't become a cynic

Be ethical

Re-read Chapter 8, "Keeping Your Toes out of Ethical Hot Water", and apply it in all aspects of your practice.

Little things that mean a lot

- Keep your cool, even when provoked
- Be courteous (remember, you can be tough without shouting or insulting people)
- Be careful
- Work hard
- If you are unsure, say so

- Establish excellent relations with court officials and employees of government agencies with whom you deal regularly
- Don't revel in the brilliance of your work when its message is negative for your client
- If you are working on something that seems to be taking a long time, or to be unlikely to help your client, say so before you run up too much of a bill
- Learn to dictate and use a computer
- Learn how to take notes extremely well
- Learn about trust accounting
- Docket your work fully, accurately and promptly
- Keep things in perspective
- Don't play politics
- Ask questions, but show you have tried to find the answer first
- Try to be a positive influence on those around you
- Exercise sound judgment in everything you do
- Recognize your limits and don't let yourself get in over your head
- Seek help from lawyers and others in your organization, classmates, lawyers in other organizations, law librarians, law teachers, the court clerks, the law society or state bar, even judges
- Last but not least, **think before you open your mouth**

Well, what should I do . . .

. . . if I pull an all-nighter and fall asleep on my keyboard the next day?

Top 14 Excuses for Sleeping on the Job:

14. I'm working smarter, not harder.
13. Wha' happened? Last thing I remember, I was cleaning my monitor with that acetone stuff.
12. Where is that darn contact lens!
11. I wasn't sleeping! I was contemplating our mission statement!

10. Whoo, boy, am I woozy. I just gave blood, you know.
9. Hey! I was just about to figure out a solution to, uh, umm . . . .Darn, now I forget!
8. Oh no! I must have gotten the decaf.
7. Boy, is that cold medicine ever long-lasting!
6. Oh no! I was just about to envision a new paradigm.
5. If it was good enough for Reagan . . .
4. So sue me, this isn't one of my high-energy times.
3. Where were you at six o'clock this morning when I was going full tilt?
2. I thought you were gone for the day.

And the best one of all:

1. Don't worry, I'm billing a client for "Reviewing the file."

Chapter 11

Planning Your Career

We all know lawyers who climb over other people to reach their career goals. They kick and scratch and bully their way to the top, and sometimes become wealthy and powerful on the way. I don't know if they are happy, but I do know that they often make the people around them miserable. Many of them are insensitive, paranoid, even sociopathic. They succeed, in part, because they find organizations that tolerate and even reward their behavior.

If this is your pathway to success, you don't need to read any further in this chapter because it doesn't contain anything of value to you. However, if you are looking for a more humanistic vision of how to succeed in the practice of law, read on.

> 66The future is not a result of choices among alternative paths offered by the present, but a place that is created—created first in the mind and will, and created next in activity. The future is not someplace you are going to but one you are creating. The paths to it are not found, but made.99
>
> —ED POLL,
> *Attorney and Law Firm Guide to the Business of Law*

Career planning

The goal of career planning is to help you to find work which brings you deep personal satisfaction. Lawyers who are truly satisfied have three characteristics:

1. They integrate their personal values into their day-to-day work experience
2. They love their work
3. They work in organizations in which they feel their values are approved

1. Integration of values and work

The lawyers who find the greatest satisfaction from practicing law are able to integrate their core **professional** and **personal** values into their day-to-day legal work.

All lawyers must aspire to the professional values that form the foundations of our ethical codes, including honesty, integrity, reliability, civility, respect for the law, loyalty and commitment to client interests, and a high regard for the interests of society. If these values are not central to your value system, you should re-evaluate your decision to practice law.

Lawyers also subscribe to a wide variety of personal values, and personal values that are central to one lawyer may be incidental or even antithetical to others. For example:

- Some lawyers value security, while others glory in risk-taking
- Some instinctively resolve conflict by compromise, while others like the thrill of gladiatorial combat
- Some are natural prosecutors, some are natural defense counsel, and some never want to see the inside of a criminal courtroom
- Some aspire to fame, while others are content with obscurity
- Some want to become very rich, a few are happy living in solidarity with the poor and most have middle-class financial aspirations somewhere in between

There is even disagreement about the basic purpose of practicing law. Some think it is to help the downtrodden, but others consider it to be to maintain social order, preserve money and property, advance the law, facilitate business transactions, or any of a large number of other socially valuable goals.

This diversity is important because it enriches our profession and gives clients choices. In practical terms, however, the range of personal values open to lawyers is not unlimited. Some values are just not compatible with a satisfying legal career, but the only way for new lawyers to find out if they are cut out for the practice of law is to try it for a while. Once they have committed themselves to a legal career, the discovery that they should be doing something else is traumatic. The good thing is, they have choices.

> Someone with a fundamental commitment to abstract intellectualizing may never achieve the pragmatism that practicing law demands. Likewise, someone who hates conflict may not be able to handle the adversarial nature of law practice.

So an important step in planning your legal career, as in all of life, is clarity about what really matters to you.

2. Work they love

Lawyers can discipline themselves to keep plugging away at work they dislike for a while—sometimes for a long while. However, if they continue too long, they lose the ability to function effectively as lawyers and human beings. A lawyer with a practice that contains an excessive amount of such work eventually becomes profoundly unhappy, even clinically depressed, with disastrous consequences both personally and professionally.

During your first two years of practice, you'll undoubtedly have to do some work you don't like, but that's part of the growth process. It's important to expose yourself to as many legal experiences as possible. Don't avoid work just because you think you may not like it; you may be surprised that corporate law, which you loved in law school, is boring, but custody cases, which you thought would be just awful, really fascinate you. Or you might have been sure that you could never be a litigator, but learn that you thrive in the courtroom.

As you develop a feel for the scope of the legal work available, start probing your own experiences to determine what kind of legal work is most satisfying to you. This is a very personal, individual process; it doesn't matter what anyone else likes or dislikes. What really matters is, do you like it? Does it make you excited about being a lawyer? Does it make you want to exclaim, "Yes! That was good! That's what it is to be a lawyer!"?

You need to dig deep and be specific. For example, if you like going to court, what excites *you* about it? Is it:

- The gamesmanship involved in matching wits with other lawyers?
- The give and take of negotiations?
- Performing in the courtroom?
- The thrill of victory?
- The intellectual challenge of organizing a complex web of facts and law into a clear and understandable framework?
- The satisfaction of championing the downtrodden and challenging the status quo?
- The satisfaction of championing the establishment and maintaining the status quo?
- The thrill of getting your name in the paper?

> As you learn more about what you like and don't like about practicing law, write your observations down. Then write down how you can shape your career to get more of what you like and less of what you don't like.

If you like office work, what brings you the most satisfaction? Is it:

- The intellectual challenge of putting together an intricate set of documents to "paper" a complex deal?
- The give and take of negotiations?

- The creative satisfaction of drafting a clear, concise contract?
- The excitement of participating in the development of a new business venture?
- The vicarious thrill of rubbing shoulders with business movers and shakers?
- The personal satisfaction of explaining a simple real estate deal or a will to "ordinary folks"?
- The gratification of advising a business client on how to structure a deal to prevent exposure to undue risk or to reduce taxes?

As you learn what you like and don't like in the practice of law, start thinking about what you need to do to develop a practice that consists entirely of clients and files you like.

3. An approving organization

Most lawyers aren't truly satisfied in their careers unless they find an organization in which their goals and values are approved.

> Switching jobs is not a sign of a failure.

There is a tremendous diversity in legal organizations. Some expect their lawyers to be, above all, excellent technicians. Others want lawyers who support and care for their clients. In some, money is an overriding concern, while in others, money takes a second place to client service. Some are extremely cautious or academic in their approach to cases; others are more daring or pragmatic.

> There is no perfect organization. You shouldn't compromise your fundamental values, but you may have to decide whether to compromise your wants and wishes to garner other benefits that can flow from being part of an organization.

Because of the gap between what people say in interviews and what actually happens in legal organizations on a day-to-day basis, it takes a while for a new lawyer to figure out what's really real in an organization. Some fit smoothly into the first organization they join, but if you don't, you need to figure out where the problem lies. If the organization doesn't support your fundamental values, you should move on. If the issues that bother you are not basic, you have the choice of staying on a while longer to see if you can bring about improvements in the situation or moving on.

Specialization

It may seem strange to discuss specialization in a book for new lawyers. After all, isn't specialization something you aspire to after many years of legal practice, involving certification by a regulatory body after extensive testing and examination of your experience?

It's true that specialist certification is reserved for more senior lawyers in those jurisdictions that have adopted it, but *de facto* specialization is now very common and is spreading rapidly in all areas of the profession. Specialized lawyers are, generally speaking, more focused, more profitable and more satisfied than their colleagues with general practices. So while I encourage young lawyers to seek out a wide range of experiences in the first couple of years of practice, I also advise them to take vigorous action to narrow their practices as soon as they are confident that they have found what they want to do as a lawyer.

There are several ways to specialize:

- In an **area of law**, such as criminal, family, securities, tax
- In a **type of legal service**, such as court or appellate representation, mediation and arbitration, research, drafting documents, negotiating
- In an **industry**, such as oil and gas, entertainment, steel, computers
- In a **market**, such as middle-class suburbanites buying and selling residential real estate, farmers and ranchers trying to avoid taxes when they pass their land onto the next generation, accountants with clients who need businesses legally organized

Each type of specialization offers an endless list of opportunities, but make sure the market you decide to go after is large enough to support another lawyer.

When you have decided on your area of concentration, you shift into marketing mode. Who controls the distribution of the work you want to do? How can you draw yourself to their attention? How can you establish a relationship with them? What issues are they interested in? Where do they gather? What do they read? How can you help them, other than by providing legal services?

It takes time for a specialist practice to evolve. You should expect to dedicate at least two years of concentrated effort before you begin to see results, and it may well take longer than that. In the meantime, what guarantee is there that you will succeed if you specialize? Well, there isn't one. You live and work in a capitalist economy. The changes that have occurred in the economics of law over the last couple of decades have forever demolished the conventional wisdom that all you have to do to succeed as a lawyer is to do good work for your clients. Now lawyers have to take risks and live or die by their decisions, just like everyone else.

And if I decide I don't want a traditional legal practice...

If you are struggling with whether you should practice law, an excellent resource is *What Can You Do With a Law Degree? A Lawyer's Guide to Career Alternatives Inside, Outside & Around the Law.* by Deborah Arron, Seattle: Niche Press, 1999.

You live in fortunate times. In the past two decades, we have witnessed the emergence of a vast array of new occupations that are well suited to people with legal training who do not want to pursue a traditional legal practice. Despite the widespread negative attitude toward lawyers, many employers view legal training as an invaluable asset in a prospective employee. Some are service occupations that support the legal profession, such as freelance research lawyers, large document litigation management specialists, paralegals, marketing consultants, headhunters, technology consultants, legal editors and many more. Others are involved in the regulation of the profession, such as discipline counsel, ethics counsel, practice management advisers and complaints mediators. New teaching opportunities have opened up outside the law schools in other university programs, community colleges, legal assistant training institutions and high schools. There are also many new opportunities for lawyers in the business, government and nonprofit sectors.

If you decide to move to a new position, consider registering with a legal headhunting agency. Headhunters are not career counselors; their clients are the employers who pay their fees, and their job is to find candidates for positions, not positions for candidates. They look for people who know what they want to do with their lives, so don't give a headhunter a resume that says, "I will do anything, as long as you pay me."

> Never give out a resume that is less than absolutely letter-perfect.

And if I decide to go out on my own ...

Lawyers are a decidedly independent lot, and many of you will decide to start your own firms. Some will be solo practices, and some will be small firms. You will be starting a new business, so you should carry out your decision in a businesslike way. Prepare a business plan that states your mission, identifies your target markets and outlines your production, marketing, personnel, financial, technology, basic office systems and organizational strategies.

If you do decide to go out on your own:

- Check to see if your law society or state bar has a law practice management assistance program that can provide you with resources to get your new firm going
- Buy a copy of Jay Foonberg's classic, *How to Start and Build a Law Practice* from the Law Practice Management Section of the American Bar Association (1-800-252-1222 or http://www.abanet.org//pm)

Job ads

When you're looking for a job, here's what those job ads really mean:

We are looking for someone who is:

Self-motivated .... Forget about mentoring, you'll be on your own

Meticulous about detail .... You do your own proofreading

Career-minded .... Female applicants better forget about having children

Experienced .... Bring a practice with you

A team leader .... Expect management responsibilities without any extra pay

Able to carry a heavy load..................... You whine, you're fired

A self-starter... Payment is a fee split based on collections

Able to work with people........................ Our senior partner has an oversized ego

Up on technology.................................. No secretary for you, plus you will be our free in-house techie

Able to work with difficult clients .... At last, we'll have someone to do our family law files!

Willing to work some overtime.............. No more often than once a night and twice on weekends

A practical problem-solver .... We haven't cracked a law book in 10 years and we don't want any one who will embarrass us

We offer:

A competitive salary............................... We are competitive because we pay less than our competition

A fast-paced practice .... We don't have time to train you

A casual work atmosphere..................... We don't pay enough to cover nice clothes

A competitive environment .... There's lots of turnover

Flexible hours.. Work 70 hours, get paid for 35

Well, what should I do?

Find a legal organization in which you can express your core personal values in your daily work, doing work you love, with the approval of the organization.

Chapter 12

Balancing the Law and Your Life

A practicing lawyer faces innumerable "should" questions:

- Which file should I work on first?
- Should I file this motion even though it probably lacks merit?
- Should I work on this file tonight or go home and watch my kid play soccer?
- Should I recommend this settlement?
- How much should I bill on this file?
- Should I work out today?
- Should I stay married?
- Should I just get drunk and forget it all?

Many conflicting voices shout out answers to these questions. The major ones belong to your clients, your peers and superiors in the legal organization in which you work, the courts, your family and friends, your colleagues in the profession, and your law society or state bar. If you are religious, you may also hear some voices from that part of your life. In this cacophony, the hardest voice to hear may be your own.

Know yourself

Your first few years of practice is a time of great personal change as your **lawyerly persona** starts to evolve. It happens to all of us.

> 66 You should not confuse your career with your life. Your friends love you anyway. Nobody cares if you can't dance well. Just get up and dance. 99
>
> —DAVE BARRY,
> *Dave Barry Turns 50*

Lawyerly persona: everything you do, consciously and unconsciously, to tell the world you are in "lawyer" mode, including your level of assertiveness, body language, facial expressions, clothes and vocabulary

You may like your new image. It may represent a pinnacle, a culmination of your whole life to that point. You experience feelings of power, presence and confidence that are quite intoxicating. You revel in your ability to analyze situations, predict outcomes and give advice. You feel glad to be a member of the legal profession and the legal organization in which you work. You look forward to the future with hope and you feel that your career is well on its way.

On the other hand, you may find the changes unsettling. Your new identity upsets you as you observe yourself doing things that you wouldn't have thought you would do. You are still trying to figure out if you really want to be a lawyer. The future is uncertain.

I still remember my first debtor examination. It was obvious that the wretched woman I was examining had nothing. She couldn't even afford a babysitter and had to bring her sickly four-year-old with her. But I was a lawyer, I was entitled to examine her and there was no way I was going to let my emotions stop me from doing my job. Slavishly following my checklist, I actually asked her if she had any gold coins. Gold coins, for crying out loud! She probably couldn't afford food for her children. It was a farce, carried on with that intense seriousness we lawyers think is so important.

Well, it took me several years to sort it out. I started with a puzzle: how could I do that? How could I subject another human being to such an indignity? It just wasn't like me. I realized that if I couldn't work out the relationship between my fundamental values and the things I was required to do as a lawyer, I would have to quit practicing law.

After a time, I realized I was expected to exercise judgment. I should not have performed the examination like a scripted actor. One look at the poor woman told me all I needed to know, and if my firm would not accept my judgment that the examination was unnecessary, I would just have to find another place to practice. It was several difficult years before I began to be comfortable as a lawyer. Eventually, however, I worked it out and am now proud to be a member of this profession.

The practice of law is not for everyone, and some new lawyers never make the transition. They find the lawyerly persona alienating, even frightening. They dislike the gap it opens up between them and the rest of world, including their friends and relatives. If they are smart, they leave the practice of law and move on. It takes courage for them to quit because there is a widespread belief that anyone who is lucky enough to receive a legal education has no business being unhappy practicing law.

Those who don't make the transition but remain as lawyers are usually profoundly unhappy. They have difficulty coping with the stress that comes from the conflict between their core values and their day-to-day work activities. They feel trapped. They get depressed. They burn out. They turn to drink and/or drugs (prescription and illicit). They come to the attention of the profession's regulatory bodies with malpractice claims, competency problems and ethical breaches. They don't feel like part of the profession because they feel they have to maintain a psychological distance to preserve their own sense of personal integrity.

Why is the profession like this?

Well, it's complicated. There are several reasons.

First, there are few natural lawyers. Most of us have to feel our way into the lawyer role.

Second, the academic criteria that got you into and through law school have very little to do with whether you will be happy practicing law. Given the irrelevance of law school admission processes and curricula to the day-to-day experience of practicing law, it's surprising that so many stay in the profession.

Third, getting your first legal job is a real throw of the dice. The chances are actually pretty remote that your first legal job will match your deep needs. If you start in the wrong job and don't take charge of your career by initiating a move, you may never find out if there is a suitable place for you in the legal profession.

Fourth, when you work in an organization, you look to the leaders to figure out how you should act. Legal organizations are usually led by very strong people. If the fundamental values of the leaders of your organization are different from yours, you will be ground between a rock and a hard place: your desire to succeed will motivate you to conform to the values of the organization, while your need to act with personal integrity will drive you to resist them. If you are not careful, you will become alienated from both the organization and yourself. If you are not strong enough to withstand the pressure to go along with "the way things are done here" when it conflicts with what you feel is right, you are a prime candidate for depression and burnout.

Fifth, the social expectations that shape lawyers are extremely powerful. You soon learn that clients, colleagues, judges, friends and relatives and the general public expect you to act in certain ways. You also learn that it easier to succeed when you conform to other peoples' ideas about how a lawyer should behave. If you don't, it confuses people. It takes a strong personality with deep personal values to respond to these pressures with integrity.

The high cost of objectivity

For most people, life is a rich, warm, messy human interplay of fact, meaning, opinion, misunderstanding, misperception, deceit, hope, fear, love, wishes, desires, likes and dislikes. Our particular claim to fame is that we are objective. We drain all the emotion out of the situation, leaving nothing but the facts and the law. We say we can see things as they are — or at least, the way other lawyers see them. We consider over-involvement as immature and lacking in professionalism.

We are objective, so we:

• Dispassionately assess our clients' cases and truthfully advise them, even when they do not want to hear what we have to say
• Act in our clients' interests even when doing so does not maximize our own benefits
• Act ethically when doing so is viewed by many as immoral (for example, by representing guilty, violent criminals)

To discharge these responsibilities, we distance ourselves from our clients and their situations. We put on a mask that is cold, unemotional, hard-nosed and analytical. That's what people pay us for, even though the way we respond to emotionally charged situations looks detached and unnatural.

Our objectivity can be dangerous to our health. It can deprive us of deep, emotionally satisfying relationships. We are particularly at risk if we let our lawyerly objectivity spill over into our personal lives. We can end up completely bereft of significant emotional attachments, particularly if people perceive us as insensitive, arrogant, intimidating, manipulative and aggressive, as they often do—accurately, I might say, in too many instances.

Objectivity can lead to loneliness, which may be amplified by unfairly hostile public attitudes toward our profession. Much of the public's dislike of lawyers comes from untrue stereotypes based on a misunderstanding of our commitment to objectivity. People resent what they perceive as our willingness to ignore and trample on emotions and relationships. The decline in civility and collegiality among lawyers also contributes to the loneliness and alienation.

It's a Catch-22 situation. Professionally, you can't reduce your commitment to objectivity. The stress experienced by lawyers who lose their objectivity far exceeds that of lawyers who maintain it. At the same time, however, if you become a purely objective, totally unemotional lawyer, you risk burnout because you will lack the deep understanding of life and people you need to be of true value to your clients. Lawyers, like all people, are multidimensional, and you need to empower personal dimensions of your life beyond your lawyerly persona. You need to learn to switch off "the lawyer thing".

In other words, you need both the objectivity and the emotion: you need to find a balance.

What is at stake?

If you stay too long in an organization that operates by basic values that are not consistent with yours, you run the risk of falling victim to what I call "The Peggy Lee Syndrome." It goes like this.

You start by grabbing the brass ring of admission to law school. You enter law school full of ideals and passion, but you quickly learn that there is another brass ring to grab: a job. You jump into the competition and land a good one.

"Wow!" you think. "This is great!"

But soon after you start your new job, you become aware of the next brass ring: making partner. All it takes is a mind-numbing, family-killing number of billable hours each year for the next seven to nine years for the opportunity to be considered for partnership, with no guarantees.

"Oh," you think. "This isn't what I thought it would be like. Well, I guess it must be the thing to do, because it's what everyone else is doing." (In fact, not everyone is, but you don't notice.)

So, you put in the hours, neglect your family, burn yourself down and make partner. Now you have to maintain your billings as high as before (it would be unseemly for a partner to bill less than an associate!), but you also have to participate in management and marketing. For this, you pay a capital contribution?

So late one night, you are driving to your heavily mortgaged home after a hard, long day at the office. Long days are the norm. You've had no actual holidays in four years. You are making great money, but you are tired and dispirited and you miss the idealistic, passionate person you were when you decided to go to law school.

Then jazz singer Peggy Lee's voice comes into your head and you hear her singing her famous song, "Is That All There Is?", and it goes through you like a knife.

It can happen to anyone

Although the above description puts the Peggy Lee Syndrome in the context of large law firm, it can happen to anyone. The essence of the malady is a dissonance between your values and the things you need to do on a day-to-day basis to succeed in the organization in which you work.

The Peggy Lee Syndrome does not happen to every lawyer. Many lawyers, probably most, find an organization in which they can practice law in a manner that is consistent with their basic goals and values. Those who don't run a serious risk of severe health problems, both mental and physical. Depression is widespread in our profession, and much of it, I'm convinced, happens in lawyers who lock themselves in careers that are bad for their health.

Questions and answers

When you ask yourself the following questions, listen for your own voice:

- What do I like most about my work? least?
- If I could stop practicing law without any financial loss, would I?
- What am I giving up to be able to practice law? Is it worth it?
- Do I look forward to going to work?
- What would I do differently if I could do it all over again?
- When I look back on the next two years, will I be proud of what I have done?
- Do I have good relationships with the people I work with? Do I trust and respect them? Do they trust and respect me?
- Does my firm practice law in a way that is consistent with my basic values?
- Is practicing law consistent with my basic values?
- Do I make a positive contribution by being a lawyer?

There are no correct answers to these questions, except answers that are right or wrong for you.

Take care...
... of yourself

What you do is important. Sometimes you will be so over-whelmed by the needs of others that you will forget that you have needs too. So please, take care of yourself:

- Take holidays—short, if not long
- Create time for solitude and reflection—meditate, pray, walk in the woods, play with your dog or cat—whatever you need to bring about spiritual regeneration
- Get organized—make lists, delegate, use technology
- Take a time management course
- Be alert to the danger signs of burnout, such as:
    - Anxiety
    - Despair, feelings of helplessness
    - Depression
    - Feelings of impotence, inferiority, loneliness, being trapped
    - Loss of confidence
    - Frustration
    - Irritability
    - Impulsiveness
    - Thoughts of suicide
- Take a dog into your office
- Take a token of your family into your office—a child's art work, a picture, a memento of a vacation
- Don't stay where you are if the only thing that keeps you there is the money
- Learn how to avoid clients and files you hate—Just say no!
- Make excellent coffee
- Eat good, nutritious food at regular times

- Eat breakfast!
- Use meals as a break from work, not an opportunity to work differently
- Control the booze, pills and cigarettes (remember, alcohol is our drug of choice)
- Exercise
- Go to bed (in other words, don't let yourself become deeply fatigued by chronically depriving yourself of however much sleep you need)

... of your family

- Take holidays with them
- Eat together
- When you're there, be there, not somewhere else
- Don't bring your lawyerly behaviors home
- Recognize when you pass your stress on—don't be a stress carrier

... of your co-workers and colleagues in the profession

- Pick partners, associates and support staff you like and respect
- Don't base your partnership on money considerations, but on fundamental values
- Ask yourself, is my attitude worth catching?
- Recognize that sometimes you must follow if other times you are to lead
- Be civil
- Support your fellow lawyers—concede and cooperate where it doesn't affect your client's rights

None of this is news. Many people have said it before.

Saying it is easy; doing it is harder; being it is hardest.

If what you feel you must say and what you feel you must do are not consistent with who you are, you need to change.

But if you are honest with yourself and create a work life in which there is coherence between your day-to-day activities and your basic values, you will achieve the essence of integrity. To me, this is what it means to *be* a professional.

Epilogue
The View from the First Lookout

Here you are at the first lookout, a narrow ledge on a steep mountain face.

Shrouded in mist far below, you can just make out where you stood a few short years ago at the bottom of the steepest learning curve you have ever climbed. Far off in the distance, you can see where you were when you began law school.

You have learned much in the last few years about the law, lawyers, clients, life in general and, most of all, about yourself. You aren't the same person you were when you started up this mountain, and it's time to pause and assess whether you want to keep climbing to the next lookout.

Law is a great profession. If you're satisfied that it is (or could be) your profession, I encourage you to keep climbing.

On behalf of the profession, let me give you a hand up.

❝So here I am, the victim of my own choices—and I'm just starting.❞

—ALLY MCBEAL

Stewart Title Guaranty Company is the right choice for title insurance. We choose to keep the lawyer at the forefront of the real estate transaction, and have designed our products around that concept. We're working with lawyers, providing tools to help keep you competitive.

Some other benefits of choosing Stewart Title:

- Gold Policies* offer superior coverage for both owner and lender.
- Full survey coverage* for both owner and lender, whether or not the property is on a Registered Plan of Subdivision.
- No hardware, software or training required. Simply choose to place your order by phone or fax.
- Competitive premiums and value added services available to Examining Counsel Program participants.
- Reduced disbursements – save your clients money. Many ancillary searches are no longer required.

* Residential Properties Up-To-Four Units

STAY COMPETITIVE IN TODAY'S CHANGING REAL ESTATE PRACTICE — *IT'S YOUR CHOICE*

Sanctity of Contract
STEWART TITLE
"Enhancing the Real Estate Closing Process"

Stewart Title Guaranty Company
150 York Street, Suite 802 • Toronto, Ontario M5H 3S5
(416) 307-3300 or 1-888-667-5151